International Students' Guide

to the

GRE®

Sentence Equivalence, Text Completion, and Vocabulary Building

Bruce Rogers

WAYZGOOSE PRESS

International Students' Guide to the GRE®: Sentence Equivalence, Text Completion, and Vocabulary Building
Copyright © 2017 by Bruce Rogers

ISBN-10: 1-938757-36-X
ISBN-13: 978-1-938757-36-5

Edited by Dorothy Zemach
Book Design by DJ Rogers Design
Published in the United States by Wayzgoose Press

Table of Contrents

Answer Key:

For a complete downloadable answer key, available as a .pdf document, please visit http://wayzgoosepress.com/greprintanswerkey

Introduction to the GRE

What is the GRE?

The GRE (**G**raduate **R**ecord **E**xaminations) is a standardized, computer-based test required by most graduate schools in North America and elsewhere for admission to either M.A. programs or Ph.D. programs. It is also accepted by a growing number of M.B.A. (graduate business school) programs, although many students who intend to study business take the GMAT exam instead. It is prepared and administered by the Educational Testing Service (ETS) in Princeton, New Jersey. ETS also prepares and administers other standardized exams, such as the SAT, the TOEFL, and the TOEIC.

The test currently (2017) costs US$205 (US$220.70 in China) and is available at testing centers most days of the year. Total testing time is three hours and 45 minutes. You can take the GRE every 21 days, up to five times a year. In parts of the world where the computer-based test is not available, a paper-based GRE is available three times a year.

Unlike most computer-based exams, the GRE allows test-takers to skip questions, change answers, and answer the questions in any order.

There are three sections of the test:

- Verbal Reasoning
- Quantitative Reasoning
- Analytical Writing

What does the GRE test?

There are three types of items in the **Verbal Reasoning Section**:

- Text Completion
- Sentence Equivalence
- Reading Comprehension

Text Completion and **Sentence Equivalence** items primarily test English vocabulary: high-level, low-frequency vocabulary.

Reading Comprehension items test a wide range of reading skills. They are based on the kinds of reading passages commonly seen in graduate-level textbooks or academic journal articles. You will take two verbal sections every time you take the GRE, both with the same type of items.

This Guide focuses on Text Completion and Sentence Equivalence items, as well as on building your vocabulary to improve your ability to answer these two item types.

The **Quantitative Reasoning Section** of the GRE tests basic math concepts up through algebra I and geometry. There are four types of items in this section:

- Quantitative Comparisons
- Multiple Choice with One Answer
- Multiple Choice with More Than One Answer
- Numeric Entry Questions

The most commonly tested topics include basic algebra, geometry, averages, ratios, number properties, exponents, square roots, and numeric problem solving. There are two quantitative sections on every GRE. (The quantitative section of the GRE is generally considered easier than the quantitative section of the GMAT.) There is an on-screen calculator you can use during this section of the test.

The **Analytical Writing Section** tests your critical thinking abilities as well as your writing skills. You must write two essays. One assesses your ability to examine an issue and develop your own convincing, well-supported argument. The other presents someone else's argument. In your response, you must analyze the author's evidence and evaluate the claims made by the author.

Test Design

Section	Number of Questions	Time
Analytical Writing • Analyze an Issue • Analyze an Argument	2 separately timed writing tasks	30 minutes per task
2 sections of Verbal Reasoning • Sentence Equivalence • Text Completion • Reading Comprehension	20 questions per section	30 minutes per section
2 Sections of Quantitative Reasoning	20 questions per section	35 minutes per section

You may also have to complete a research section – an extra verbal or an extra quantitative section – that is not scored.

Choosing Answers

Work as quickly as possible. Your score depends on how many items you answer correctly. (Each item has the same value.) There is no penalty for incorrect answers, so you should always guess. When possible, however, you should avoid "taking a shot in the dark" (i.e., guessing blindly). Use the process of elimination to get rid of answer choices that are obviously wrong or that just seem wrong in order to improve your chances of making a correct guess. Then, if you have a hunch – if you think, for some reason, (D) is the best of the remaining answers – choose (D). If you have no idea, choose any remaining answer and go on, or leave it blank and come back to it later.

One good strategy is to go through the Verbal section and answer the questions that are easiest for you and skip the ones that are more difficult, and then go back and work on the harder ones after your first pass. The computer-based GRE has a function called the Review Screen that makes this easy to do. As you work through a section, you can mark questions that you had problems with and then go to the Review Screen after your first pass. The Review Screen indicates whether you have answered a question or left it incomplete. It also indicates if you marked it as an item you wanted to look at later (whether you answered the question or not) and has a "Return to question" that takes you back to the question you marked. Remember, you can always change an answer as long as it is in the section that you are working on.

You can work on only one section of the test at a time, and you must complete it within the allotted time. When time is up for one section, you can't return to it. When there is only a minute or so remaining, use the Review Screen to go to all the unanswered questions and take a guess, even if you don't have time to read the question. Don't leave any questions unanswered.

Vocabulary

This guide concentrates on Sentence Equivalence and Text Completion. These two item types basically test advanced vocabulary. In the long term, the best way to learn unfamiliar words is by reading and by using the target vocabulary in your writing and speaking. In the short-term, however, you will have to memorize words from a list of high-frequency GRE words, such as the ones in the Vocabulary Building section of this book.

Most of the words tested in these two sections are nouns, adjectives, and verbs. Short but somewhat unfamiliar words (*apt, laud, goad, irk, woo, mar*) often appear. Sometimes you may see two- to five-word phrases as answer choices in the Text Completion section.

Some of the words have common meanings, but they also have less familiar definitions. For example, the noun *pedestrian* (meaning a person who walks) is a fairly common word. However, *pedestrian*, when used as an adjective, has a less familiar meaning. It can mean ordinary or commonplace.

The following types of words will generally NOT be tested:

A. Nouns that describe concrete things and the names of animals, plants, etc. (*encyclopedia, giraffe, skyscraper, propeller, submarine, geranium, toaster, overcoat*)

B. Proper nouns and adjectives; i.e., words that start with a capital letter (names of places, people, etc. *Chicago, European, Sunday, the Civil War, Steve Jobs, Mercedes Benz*)

C. Words that are used only in specific fields, such as law or medicine (*kyphosis, constructivist, pentameter, appendicitis, pixel, adjudication, geosyncline*)

D. Structure words or signal words (*therefore, although, because*)

Exercise:

If you think these words are likely to appear as possible answer choices in Sentence Equivalence or Text Completion items, mark these words YES. If not, mark these words NO. Be ready to explain why you think they might or might not appear. (Look up any unfamiliar words.)

___ 1. elevator

___ 2. ginkgo

___ 3. robust

___ 4. truculent

___ 5. goggles

___ 6. Oriental

___ 7. homeostasis

___ 8. disingenuous

___ 9. epidermis

___ 10. meticulous

___ 11. hippopotamus

___ 12. however

Preview Test

Sentence Equivalence: Select the **TWO** answer choices that fit the meaning of the sentence and produce two sentences that are alike in meaning.

1. While all bookkeeping systems can be useful, all have certain_____.

    (A) complexities
    (B) attributes
    (C) drawbacks
    (D) withdrawals
    (E) demands
    (F) disadvantages

2. Rube Goldberg was a cartoonist who drew diagrams of extremely complicated _____ designed to accomplish very simple tasks.

    (A) contraptions
    (B) projects
    (C) gadgets
    (D) accessories
    (E) instructions
    (F) materials

3. A person who has a small appetite is said to "eat like a bird," but in reality, some birds, such as cormorants, have _____ appetites.

    (A) dismaying
    (B) ravenous
    (C) questionable
    (D) moderate
    (E) voracious
    (F) legendary

4. Considered one of the world's finest tapestries, the famed Lady and the Unicorn Tapestry, which hangs in a museum in Paris, has a somewhat _____ history.

    (A) mysterious
    (B) conventional
    (C) suspicious
    (D) enigmatic
    (E) ambivalent
    (F) banal

5. The director expected the test audience to enthusiastically approve of his newest film, but most of them had, at best, a _____ response.

    (A) fervent
    (B) craven
    (C) convoluted
    (D) lukewarm
    (E) zealous
    (F) tepid

6. Though some people learn a language best through formal academic instruction, others seem to be able to _____ language through contact with native speakers.

    (A) interpret
    (B) assimilate
    (C) adapt
    (D) absorb
    (E) extricate
    (F) modify

Text Completion: Select **ONE** entry from each column to fill in the corresponding blanks in a way that provides the best completion for the text.

7. An umbra is a shadow's darkest central point, from which all light is _____.

(A) retracted
(B) diffused
(C) excluded
(D) redirected
(E) imported

8. Aspirin can (i) _____ pain, reduce fever, and it is believed that, in low doses, it can (ii) _____ heart attacks.

Blank (i)	Blank (ii)
(A) engender	(D) forestall
(B) alleviate	(E) simulate
(C) repudiate	(F) bolster

9. In 2008, scientists discovered a 50 million-year-old fossil of a flat fish that was an (i) _____ species between primitive flat fish, which had one eye on either side of their heads, and (ii) _____ species of flat fish, such as flounders, which have both eyes on one side of their heads.

Blank (i)	Blank (ii)
(A) unknown	(D) modern
(B) ambiguous	(E) extinct
(C) intermediate	(F) related

10. Troubadours were (i) _____ French musicians who travelled from village to village in medieval times, playing songs, reciting poetry, and (ii) _____ news from other towns.

Blank (i)	Blank (ii)
(A) itinerant	(D) extrapolating
(B) morose	(E) lamenting
(C) insular	(F) disseminating

11. In science, the stereotypical image of scientific geniuses making discoveries while working (i) _____ has given way to a more (ii) _____ model, in which research is done by teams, which are often made up of researchers from different disciplines.

Blank (i)	Blank (ii)
(A) solo	(D) collaborative
(B) with alacrity	(E) haphazard
(C) arduously	(F) contemplative

6. The rivalry between the Airbus A380 and the Boeing 787 Dreamliner pits two companies with fundamentally different products and opposite visions of the future. The Airbus A380 is (i) _____ plane that can carry 550 to 800 passengers. It is built around the assumption that airlines will continue to fly smaller planes on shorter routes (spokes) into a few large hubs, then onward to the next hub. However, Boeing does not accept the current hub-and-spoke model as a given. More and more, airlines fly medium-sized planes such as the 787 on frequent point-to-point routes, and there is no sign that this trend is (ii) _____. Not long ago, it appeared as if Airbus was (iii) _____ this hard-fought competition, but with the 787, it now appears that Boeing may pull off one of the greatest reversals of business fortunes.

Blank (i)	Blank (ii)	Blank (iii)
(A) a colossal	(D) burgeoning	(G) gaining the upper hand in
(B) a lucrative	(E) mitigating	(H) walking away from
(C) an audacious	(F) abating	(I) failing to keep up in

Sentence Equivalence

Design

Each Sentence Equivalence item consists of a sentence (called "the stem") with a blank representing a word or phrase that has been omitted. Below the sentence are six choices: A, B, C, D, E, F. Your job is to choose the two options that create two logical sentences with the same meaning. The options that you choose must therefore be synonyms or words with very similar definitions. You must always choose two answers for each item, and if one of your choices is incorrect, your answer is incorrect. (There is no partial credit.)

Almost all items fit into the stem grammatically. This section does not test grammar directly. An understanding of the grammar of the sentence is often important, however.

Techniques

A. Look for key CONTENT words that point toward the right answer.

For example, consider this item:
The woman told the man that he looked _____.

    (A) healthy
    (B) ill
    (C) wealthy
    (D) fit
    (E) sick
    (F) handsome

There are no words in the stem that help you choose an answer. This would NOT be a good GRE item.

Now look again:

The doctor told the patient that he looked _____.

      (A) healthy
      (B) ill
      (C) wealthy
      (D) fit
      (E) sick
      (F) handsome

This is still not a good item, because any one of these answers *could* be correct; a doctor might tell a patient that he looked any of these ways. However, changing the word *woman* to *doctor* and *man* to *patient* gives us a certain context clue, and choices (A) and (D) or (B) and (E) are now more likely answers because they are related to health.

B. Look for key FUNCTION (STRUCTURE) words that point toward the right answer.

Consider this item:

Although the doctor told the patient that he looked _____, the patient said that he still didn't feel well.

      (A) healthy
      (B) ill
      (C) wealthy
      (D) fit
      (E) sick
      (F) handsome

The signal word *although* shows contrast or opposition. Therefore, we can assume that the correct answer will stand in contrast to the idea of not feeling well, and therefore (A) and (D) are the best options. This is now a legitimate GRE item. Through a combination of content words and structure words, you can figure out the correct answers. (However, you won't see any items on the real test quite as easy as this one.)

Here are some important structure signal words:

Contrast

although	in contrast	on the other hand
but	in spite of	rather than
despite	instead of	while
even though	on the contrary	yet

Other words can also show contrast, but in an indirect way.

a departure from	in theory ... in practice	paradoxically
amazingly	ironically	seem to be
appear to be	on the surface	surprisingly
generally	outwardly	typically
illogical	overtly	unexpectedly
in reality		

These words may show a contrast between how something *looks* and how it really is.

Example
Outwardly, he seemed calm, but anyone who really knew him realized that he was actually quite _____. (*anxious, nervous*)

They may also show contrast between how something *usually* seems and the way it looks at a certain time.

Example
The child's handwriting is *typically* sloppy and difficult to read, but the handwriting on this note is _____. (*legible, neat*)

They may also show the difference between something that is expected and something that is out of the ordinary.

Example

Having been told again and again that the director was cold and distant, we were *amazed* when she greeted us _____ as we stepped into her office. (*cordially, warmly*)

Cause and Effect

because	so ... that	resulting in
is the result of	since	as
because of	if ... then	due to

Example

Because of their amazing abilities to complete tasks, dolphins are considered very _____ creatures. (*intelligent, smart*)

Addition/Support

and	together with
also	in addition to
as well as	too
both ... and	besides
along with	not only ... but also

Examples

for instance	such as	for example

Similarity

like

alike

similar

Difference

unlike

different from

to

Alternatives

or   either ... or   otherwise

C. Watch for "reversers" that change the direction of sentences and the kind of word that you are looking for.

These reversers include negative words and phrases such as *not, no, not as, never, hardly, seldom*, and words such as *without, lacking*, and *less*.

Consider this item:

Henry thought the experiment would be difficult to perform, but it turned out to be _____.

    (A) simple
    (B) challenging
    (C) exceptional
    (D) straightforward
    (E) boring
    (F) complicated

The content word *difficult* and the structure word *but*, indicating contrast, tell us that the word that fits in the blank will have the opposite meaning of *difficult*, so choices (A) and (D) would logically fit into the blank. However, what happens if we add a reverser to the sentence?

Henry thought the experiment would be difficult to perform, but it turned out to be not nearly as _____ as he had thought.

  (A) simple
  (B) challenging
  (C) exceptional
  (D) straightforward
  (E) boring
  (F) complicated

Now, because of the reverser *not nearly*, the correct answer will have the SAME meaning as *difficult*, so choices (B) and (F) are correct.

D. It will often be useful to break down answer choices into negative, positive, and neutral words.

If you can determine from the key content and function words that a negative word is needed, for example, you can eliminate neutral and positive words.

Look at this item:
Although the province of Astonia is famous for its gorgeous landscapes, the abandoned industrial areas around the capital city are quite _____.

  (A) scenic
  (B) peaceful
  (C) grim
  (D) featureless
  (E) unsafe
  (F) unattractive

The content word *gorgeous* means "beautiful," and the word *although* indicates contrast, so the correct answers will have a negative meaning to contrast with the positive meaning of the word *gorgeous*. Choices (A) and (B) have positive meanings, and choice (D) has a neutral meaning. The correct answers are (C) and (F), which are both negative words. Choice (E) also has a negative meaning, but it is not in contrast with the word *gorgeous*, and it doesn't have a synonym.

Note that choice (A)—*scenic*—is an antonym of the correct answer. You will often see one or more words that have meanings that are the opposite of the correct answer.

E. If you don't understand some of the vocabulary in the sentence stem, try to use context clues to help you figure out the meaning of the unknown words.

Consider this sentence again:

Although the province of Astonia is famous for its gorgeous landscapes, the abandoned industrial areas around the capital city are quite _____.

It is definitely helpful to know the meaning of the word *gorgeous* when answering this item. But suppose you have no idea what this word means? Again, we know that the information in the first clause is in contrast with the information in the second clause. The second clause mentions *abandoned industrial areas*, which are typically not very attractive. So it is possible to guess that *gorgeous* means "attractive."

Let's look at another example:

Works by novice writers, such as Hemingway's early short stories, are often far less _____ than those written during the author's mature stage.

    (A) polished
    (B) exciting
    (C) popular
    (D) sophisticated
    (E) restrained
    (F) chaotic

Again, it is helpful to know the meaning of key words in the stem—in this case *novice*. If you don't know the meaning of this word (it means "beginner"), you can probably guess it, because when an author writes *early short stories*, he or she is a beginner. Also, a contrast is set up between the word *novice* and *mature*, and this could also help you figure out a definition for the word *novice*. (Answers: A/D)

F. Use the Process of Elimination.

There may be some words that you are not familiar with that you cannot eliminate. On the other hand, there may be words that you are sure are not correct, or that you think are not correct. If you can eliminate one or two words, you will be able to make a better guess.

G. When you are attacking a Sentence Equivalence item, you need to use two tactics.

First, guess what the missing words might be by using content and function words (Steps A and B). Then look for synonyms among the six answer choices. Why? Because to create two sentences that are equivalent, the two correct missing words must have the same meaning—or at least quite similar meanings.

It is important to realize, however, that using only ONE of these two techniques may not be enough on its own to determine a correct answer. Why not?

1. More than two answers may fit logically into the blank, but one or more of them may not have a synonym.

Consider this item:

In the early twentieth century, many U.S. cities had very _____ systems of urban transportation utilizing trolley cars, but by the 1950s, these had mostly been replaced by buses.

  (A) inexpensive
  (B) speedy
  (C) effective
  (D) picturesque
  (E) complex
  (F) efficient

Choices (A) and (B) may be considered logical options to replace the blank, but neither word has a synonym. Choices (C) and (F) are logical AND they are synonymous.

2. There may be more than one pair of synonyms among the answer choices, but only one pair fits logically into the blank.

Look at this item:

What economists and game-theorists call a *pareto optimal* solution is a "win-win" outcome for a problem that is _____ to all the parties involved.

    (A) beneficial
    (B) distasteful
    (C) objectionable
    (D) favorable
    (E) legitimate
    (F) practicable

Choices (B) and (C) are synonyms. These two words indicate that the solution does not please any of the parties. However, because a "pareto optimal" solution is described as a "win-win" outcome, it must help all the parties. Choices (A) and (D) are also synonyms, AND they fit into the context of the sentence because both words mean "helpful."

So remember: To be correct, the two answer choices must be more or less synonymous, and they must logically complete the sentence. As a final step, read the sentence again with your two choices in place to make sure that the two sentences you have created are both logical and that they have similar meanings.

Exercise 1:

<u>Underline</u> the pairs of synonyms in these lists of words. In some cases there may be two sets of synonyms; <u>double underline</u> the second set.

1. burnish	unite	reveal	polish	refuse	tarnish
2. revive	inundate	decorate	compromise	incite	flood
3. arduous	grueling	persistent	ardent	zealous	envious
4. fatuous	slothful	noisome	loud	disgusting	foolish
5. vague	stylish	elaborate	outmoded	perennial	fashionable
6. desiccated	restive	dehydrated	rude	tranquil	boorish
7. enervate	restrict	oversee	weaken	engender	supervise

8. lucky	gaudy	senseless	flashy	separate	romantic
9. effortless	perilous	elegant	dangerous	random	haphazard
10. criticize	banal	deface	commonplace	mar	inspire

Exercise 2:

<u>Underline</u> function (structure) words that may help you determine which word could be used in place of the blank. Circle content words that may help you determine which word could be used in place of the blank. If there are any reversers, <u>double underline</u> them. Then think of a word that might logically complete the sentence.

Example:

Although critics seldom care for musical comedies, audiences find them _____.

<u>Although</u> critics <u>seldom</u> care for musical comedies, audiences find them <u>entertaining</u>.

1. Since they occur suddenly, and since they are so powerful, avalanches can be very _____.

2. Professor Newsome is not only a good lecturer; she is also _____ advisor.

3. Despite the _____ skies, the eclipse was not completely invisible.

4. Everyone said that Mr. Ralston was rude and difficult to get along with; surprisingly, he treated us _____.

5. Octopuses have an _____ appearance, but they are not at all dangerous to humans.

6. Ironically, the employee who had the least training and least experience was the most _____.

7. Overtly, this language is not difficult to learn, yet some elements of its grammar are extremely _____ .

8. Unlike his brother Ron, who is seldom very outgoing, Sam is quite _____.

In each of the Sentence Equivalence drills, the items tend to become progressively more difficult. The first few items are easier than the last few items in each drill. However, most of the items in the drills tend to be somewhat less difficult than those found on the actual exam.

Sentence Equivalence Drill 1

Select the **TWO** answer choices that fit the meaning of the sentence and produce two sentences that are alike in meaning.

1. Outwardly the most _____ of people, he had a sentimental side to his personality that only his family and his closest friends were aware of.

   (A) extroverted
   (B) practical
   (C) romantic
   (D) pragmatic
   (E) demonstrative
   (F) ebullient

2. Warned by initial reports of widespread destruction in the downtown area, relief workers were pleased to find far less _____ than they had been led to believe.

   (A) anarchy
   (B) damage
   (C) panic
   (D) reconstruction
   (E) incompetence
   (F) devastation

3. The most _____ matters on the agenda will be discussed today, but less important matters will be taken up at next Tuesday's meeting.

   (A) urgent
   (B) pressing
   (C) annoying
   (D) covert
   (E) aggravating
   (F) entertaining

4. The protestors denounced the testing of drugs on animals in spite of the _____ information that the tests provide for scientists.

    (A) invaluable
    (B) worthless
    (C) meaningless
    (D) vital
    (E) mediocre
    (F) pointless

5. A business traveler to our city recently commented on the _____ he had seen on the streets, a departure from the cleanliness he had observed on a trip here several years before.

    (A) poverty
    (B) litter
    (C) congestion
    (D) commerce
    (E) trash
    (F) conflict

6. The _____ theft of the *Mona Lisa* from the Louvre in 1911 was one of the most spectacular crimes in the history of art.

    (A) daring
    (B) cunning
    (C) futile
    (D) audacious
    (E) puzzling
    (F) failed

7. The pygmy owl of the western United States is only about six inches (15 cm.) in length, but it is remarkably _____, attacking far larger creatures.

    (A) diminutive
    (B) greedy
    (C) fierce
    (D) ferocious
    (E) swift
    (F) tiny

8. Though the film's opening scenes were quite _____, it soon degenerated into another predictable action movie.

    (A) shocking
    (B) uninteresting
    (C) inexplicable
    (D) significant
    (E) auspicious
    (F) promising

9. The term *feedback* was originally part of the _____ of electrical engineering with a highly restricted meaning, but it has come to have a much broader definition.

    (A) jargon
    (B) details
    (C) background
    (D) classification
    (E) lexicon
    (F) fundamentals

10. One distinguishing characteristic of James Joyce's remarkable novel *Ulysses* is his unfailing attention to the _____ details of everyday life in Ireland in the early twentieth century.

    (A) superfluous
    (B) extraordinary
    (C) memorable
    (D) quotidian
    (E) banal
    (F) quaint

11. Cheetahs are the _____ of all land animals, with top speeds of up to 70 miles (112 kilometers) per hour.

    (A) most ruthless
    (B) fleetest
    (C) swiftest
    (D) wildest
    (E) most famous
    (F) most exotic

12. According to an account written by Giorgio Vasari, in 1431, Italian artist Fra Lippo Lippi was _____ and enslaved by Barbary pirates, but his skill as a portrait painter helped him win his eventual freedom.

    (A) admired
    (B) interrupted
    (C) abducted
    (D) captured
    (E) inspired
    (F) liberated

Sentence Equivalence Drill 2

Select the **TWO** answer choices that fit the meaning of the sentence and produce two sentences that are alike in meaning.

1. Despite his team's three recent losses, the coach seems _____ and remains optimistic about Saturday's match.

   (A) uncertain
   (B) inept
   (C) undaunted
   (D) inattentive
   (E) sanguine
   (F) qualified

2. While it is well known that many of the operators of games at carnival booths use _____ to separate customers from their money, there are always people who are willing to try their luck.

   (A) chicanery
   (B) lassitude
   (C) compliance
   (D) complexity
   (E) trickery
   (F) sincerity

3. Because of its _____ population, the town of Greendale must build new schools and roads.

   (A) burnishing
   (B) dwindling
   (C) burgeoning
   (D) mushrooming
   (E) welcoming
   (F) hospitable

4. Although not exactly a _____, Evelyn loves to hunt for bargains and never makes unnecessary purchases.

   (A) penny-pincher
   (B) pauper
   (C) miser
   (D) imposter
   (E) trailblazer
   (F) philanthropist

5. In his 1962 book, *Night Comes to the Cumberlands*, Harry Caudill called attention to the _____ of Appalachia, one of the poorest regions of the United States.

   (A) history
   (B) woes
   (C) plight
   (D) beliefs
   (E) customs
   (F) appeal

6. With the passage of the Soil Conservation Act of 1936, farmers were paid by the federal government to leave their land _____ or to plant crops such as timothy that put nitrogen back into the soil.

   (A) fertile
   (B) unoccupied
   (C) fallow
   (D) depleted
   (E) abandoned
   (F) uncultivated

7. Running a marathon is difficult in the best of circumstances, but it is particularly _____ to run a long race when the weather is hot and humid.

   (A) exhaustive
   (B) grueling
   (C) energizing
   (D) thrilling
   (E) enervating
   (F) invigorating

8. The other employees were amazed when Mr. Wilkins, who always seemed the meekest and most diffident person on the staff, had the _____ to storm into his boss's office and demand a raise.

   (A) thoughtfulness
   (B) anxiety
   (C) frightfulness
   (D) timidity
   (E) effrontery
   (F) temerity

9. Ms. Hagstrom was _____ business news broadcasts, and would become anxious if she didn't watch several a day.

   (A) allergic to
   (B) amused by
   (C) addicted to
   (D) hooked on
   (E) oblivious to
   (F) offended by

10. Jules Verne's 1865 novel *From the Earth to the Moon* turned out to be remarkably _____; many of the imagined aspects of that fictional flight were echoed by actual features of the Apollo mission to the Moon in 1969.

   (A) prescient
   (B) inaccurate
   (C) fanciful
   (D) humorous
   (E) prophetic
   (F) controversial

11. Although the siblings sometimes _____ about trivial personal matters, they cooperate fully when managing the family business.

   (A) interact
   (B) consult
   (C) quibble
   (D) agree
   (E) bicker
   (F) reflect

12. The fact that objects as massive as continents are constantly in motion seems so _____ that, when the idea of continental drift was first proposed by Alfred Wegener in 1912, few people took it seriously.

   (A) implausible
   (B) feasible
   (C) preposterous
   (D) subtle
   (E) abstract
   (F) hilarious

Sentence Equivalence Drill 3

Select the TWO answer choices that fit the meaning of the sentence and produce two sentences that are alike in meaning.

1. There are 88 keys on _____ piano, but some special types have smaller or larger keyboards.

   (A) an antiquated
   (B) a standard
   (C) an exotic
   (D) an enhanced
   (E) a conventional
   (F) a modified

2. One of earliest _____ of the U.S. space program was the discovery of the Van Allen radiation belts in 1958.

   (A) triumphs
   (B) restrictions
   (C) controversies
   (D) demands
   (E) objectives
   (F) successes

3. Choreographer Lois Fuller created a number of _____ dances, including the breathtaking fire dance.

   (A) original
   (B) informal
   (C) striking
   (D) capricious
   (E) dramatic
   (F) symbolic

4. Social activist Dorothy Day established a number of hospitality houses to feed the hungry, house the homeless, and provide other necessary services for _____ people.

    (A) indolent
    (B) itinerant
    (C) complacent
    (D) destitute
    (E) wandering
    (F) indigent

5. The poet e e cummings made up his own words, _____ many of the conventions of spelling and typography, and re-invented rules of grammar, but despite their nontraditional form, cummings' poems came to be popular with many readers.

    (A) relished
    (B) flouted
    (C) spurned
    (D) disguised
    (E) employed
    (F) induced

6. Stella Adler played _____ role in the development of the Method school of acting and her acting workshop in New York produced such distinguished alumni as Marlon Brando and Robert de Niro.

    (A) a pioneering
    (B) a discreet
    (C) a crucial
    (D) an encompassing
    (E) a pervasive
    (F) a pivotal

7. The muffler on a car reduces engine noise by conducting exhaust gases around a series of obstacles called baffles, which _____ the noise.

    (A) echo
    (B) soak up
    (C) deflect
    (D) absorb
    (E) leak out
    (F) turn up

8. The Beatles took the inspiration for their songs from _____ sources: pop music, the blues, jazz, classical, Indian music, and even country music.

    (A) archaic
    (B) disparate
    (C) eclectic
    (D) witty
    (E) mundane
    (F) inaccessible

9. Thomas Paine's pamphlet *Common Sense* is written in a brisk style and contains many _____ quotations that bolster his ideas.

    (A) fitting
    (B) odd
    (C) classical
    (D) apt
    (E) brief
    (F) trite

10. The island of Britain was the last territory that the Roman Empire established _____ over, and it was the first to be abandoned by the Roman legions.

    (A) dogma
    (B) assault
    (C) hegemony
    (D) dominion
    (E) demand
    (F) nostalgia

11. The inventor Nikola Tesla developed more and more _____ after he was struck by a taxi cab in 1937; for example, he felt compelled to feed the pigeons in front of the New York Public Library, and he would bring sick and injured pigeons back to his hotel room to try to nurse them back to health.

    (A) eccentricities
    (B) differences
    (C) peculiarities
    (D) struggles
    (E) contraptions
    (F) hazards

12. Sheep can be _____ liquid chemicals to eliminate ticks and other external parasites.

    (A) injected with
    (B) sprayed with
    (C) immersed in
    (D) dipped in
    (E) herded through
    (F) suspended above

Sentence Equivalence Drill 4

Select the **TWO** answer choices that fit the meaning of the sentence and produce two sentences that are alike in meaning.

1. Often sitting through cabinet meetings without saying a single word, the famously _____ President Calvin Coolidge was nicknamed "Silent Cal."

    (A) taciturn
    (B) garrulous
    (C) verbose
    (D) sociable
    (E) irascible
    (F) laconic

2. The term "robber barons" was used in the 19th century to describe _____ businessmen who amassed vast amounts of wealth using questionable practices.

    (A) powerful
    (B) illegitimate
    (C) inspirational
    (D) rapacious
    (E) clever
    (F) greedy

3. In the 1950s, at the _____ of the Baby Boom, nearly 25 per cent of all boys and girls were given one of the ten most popular names, but today, only about 8 per cent of all children have one of the most popular names.

    (A) peak
    (B) dawn
    (C) time
    (D) height
    (E) maturity
    (F) conclusion

4. The 16ᵗʰ century Japanese poet Basho made a living as a writer and a teacher, but he _____ the social, urban life of the established literary circles and was inclined to wander throughout the countryside.

   (A) described
   (B) renounced
   (C) cherished
   (D) discredited
   (E) admonished
   (F) spurned

5. At the 1900 New York Auto Show, the audience favored electrically powered cars over gasoline or kerosene powered cars because they were quiet and easy to handle and did not produce _____ fumes.

   (A) smelly
   (B) excessive
   (C) fragrant
   (D) invisible
   (E) malodorous
   (F) vapid

6. Many Roman politicians maintained villas in _____ areas to escape the pressures and distractions of life in the capital of the Empire.

   (A) rustic
   (B) urban
   (C) rural
   (D) defensible
   (E) exotic
   (F) uncharted

7. The outlaw Jesse James, a legendary bank robber, train robber, and gunfighter, was a celebrity even before his death, but he became an even more _____ figure after he appeared as a character in several of the lurid "dime novels" of the 1890s.

   (A) diligent
   (B) complaisant
   (C) infamous
   (D) celebrated
   (E) notorious
   (F) unseemly

8. In an effort to counter the loss of languages in India, which has more endangered languages than any other country, linguist Ganesh Devy is attempting to at least record these tongues before they _____.

   (A) aspire
   (B) disappear
   (C) evolve
   (D) default
   (E) vanish
   (F) retire

9. Researchers at the Museum of the Rockies have theorized that a well-known type of dinosaur, the triceratops, may not have been a distinct species, but rather the _____ form of another dinosaur, known as the torosaurus.

   (A) juvenile
   (B) unknown
   (C) fossilized
   (D) fragmented
   (E) analogous
   (F) immature

10. The Navigation Acts were a series of laws passed by the British Parliament that were designed to _____ trade between Britain's North American colonies and other European powers.

    (A) curb
    (B) restrict
    (C) negotiate
    (D) protect
    (E) apprise
    (F) stimulate

11. So strong was the Persian _____ for turning everyday expressions into poems that one can encounter forms of poetry in almost every classical work, whether from Persian literature, science, or metaphysics, and the ability to write in verse form was a pre-requisite for any scholar.

    (A) distaste
    (B) penchant
    (C) quirk
    (D) antipathy
    (E) knack
    (F) response

12. The _____ of surviving the next election partially explains why many politicians are so short-sighted, but it does not explain why they are more short-sighted than corporate managers, who are also constantly in danger of losing their jobs.

    (A) mandate
    (B) anomaly
    (C) hegemony
    (D) imperative
    (E) possibility
    (F) consequence

Sentence Equivalence Drill 5

Select the **TWO** answer choices that fit the meaning of the sentence and produce two sentences that are alike in meaning.

1. As global temperatures rise, glaciers all over the world continue to _____.

   (A) thaw
   (B) form
   (C) advance
   (D) dazzle
   (E) evolve
   (F) melt

2. Often performed by children, the Virginia Reel is _____ dance usually accompanied by fast-paced music.

   (A) a traditional
   (B) a stately
   (C) a lively
   (D) an expressive
   (E) a spirited
   (F) a popular

3. This is no time for _____; this is a serious matter, and we must give it our undivided attention.

   (A) solemnity
   (B) levity
   (C) haste
   (D) brevity
   (E) frivolity
   (F) reflection

4. In Colonial North America, physicians were generally poorly paid and poorly trained, and they were not usually _____ by the public.

    (A) vilified
    (B) respected
    (C) esteemed
    (D) castigated
    (E) eschewed
    (F) ridiculed

5. When Admiral Jacob Roggeveen visited Easter Island in 1722, he wrote that there were hundreds of the mysterious statues known as Moai standing upright; but when Captain Cook came to Easter Island in 1774, he reported that only nine statues were still standing, and that all the rest had been _____.

    (A) toppled
    (B) dragged away
    (C) dismantled
    (D) propped up
    (E) enhanced
    (F) knocked over

6. Many law firms try to _____ top-ranking graduates of prestigious law schools with promises of high salaries and quick advancement.

    (A) goad
    (B) appease
    (C) dupe
    (D) woo
    (E) recruit
    (F) dismiss

7. Julius Caesar is known not only for his military and political leadership, but also for his _____ style of writing.

   (A) sensational
   (B) derivative
   (C) lucid
   (D) understated
   (E) impassioned
   (F) articulate

8. Except for the film *Slaughterhouse 5*, which he found brilliant, Kurt Vonnegut considered all the other movies made from his novels _____.

   (A) homogenous
   (B) mendacious
   (C) unfathomable
   (D) execrable
   (E) tolerable
   (F) wretched

9. Goldbach's Conjecture, first proposed in 1742, is one of the oldest and best-known unsolved _____ in number theory and, in fact, in all of mathematics.

   (A) conundrums
   (B) puzzles
   (C) contentions
   (D) paragons
   (E) catalysts
   (F) implosions

10. As a neo-classical architect, Thomas Jefferson was inspired by the Roman style of architecture, as seen in the buildings he designed at the University of Virginia, whereas Charles Bullfinch tended to _____ the English style of architecture.

   (A) emulate
   (B) stigmatize
   (C) modify
   (D) follow
   (E) instigate
   (F) extrapolate

11. As the pace of technological change quickens, many products that seemed revolutionary just five years ago now seem _____.

   (A) obnoxious
   (B) obsolete
   (C) pioneering
   (D) eclectic
   (E) antiquated
   (F) innovative

12. In the fall of 2008, the prices of stocks on markets around the world began to _____ in a way they had not done since the Great Depression of the 1930s.

   (A) plunge
   (B) flip
   (C) rebound
   (D) plummet
   (E) fluctuate
   (F) stabilize

Text Completion

Design

The texts consist of from one to five sentences. There will be from one to three blanks in the text, and you must choose appropriate words or short phrases to fill those blanks.

If there is one blank, there will be five possible answer choices.

1. Xx xxx x xxxxxx _____ xxxxxxxxxxxxx xxx xxxx.

(A)
(B)
(C)
(D)
(E)

If there are two blanks, there will be six answer choices—three for each blank.

2. Xxxx x xxxxxxxxx (i) _____ xxx xxxxxxxxxx xxxxx xxxxx x (ii) _____.

Blank (i)	Blank (ii)
(A)	(D)
(B)	(E)
(C)	(F)

If there are three blanks, there are nine answer choices—again, three for each blank.

3. Xxxx xx xxx (i) _____ xxx xxxxxx (ii) _____ xxx xxxxxxxxxx xxxx (iii) _____.

Blank (i)	Blank (ii)	Blank (iii)
(A)	(D)	(G)
(B)	(E)	(H)
(C)	(F)	(I)

You must correctly fill each blank. As in Sentence Equivalence problems, if one of your choices is incorrect, your answer is incorrect. (There is no partial credit.)

The answer choices for one blank may be dependent on the choice for another blank; i.e., selecting a correct response for one blank cannot be determined without considering the answer choice for another blank or blanks.

Example

Just as a misanthrope is known as a person who dislikes other people, a (i) _____ is known as someone who (ii) _____ others.

Blank (i)	Blank (ii)
(A) quitter	(D) instructs
(B) traditionalist	(E) assists
(C) philanthropist	(F) understands

The answers are (C) and (E). The first part of the sentence defines a misanthrope; the second part of the sentence defines another type of person. A *quitter* is a person who does not finish tasks. None of the words in blank (ii) are related to *quitter*. A *traditionalist* is a person who follows customs and the old ways of doing things. None of the words in blank (ii) are related to this kind of person. A *philanthropist* is a person who is generous to and helps people, often by donating money to them. The word *assists* is therefore the correct choice. You need to consider all the possible options for both blanks to answer this item because the answers are dependent on each other.

Text Completion items are similar in many ways to Sentence Equivalence. Both require you to use your knowledge of vocabulary (often quite advanced vocabulary) and your understanding of the logic of what you read in order to complete a short text. Both share the same problems and pitfalls.

You will also use many of the same tools and techniques for solving Text Completion problems.

A. As in Sentence Equivalence, this section does not test grammar directly. An understanding of the grammar of the sentence is again important, however.

B. Both function (structure) words and content words can serve as sign-posts that can point you towards the correct answers.

C. Watch for "reversers" (such as negative words).

Consider this sentence:
Although always kind to strangers, Jennifer is _____ to her friends.

In this sentence, because of the contrast word "although," the word in the blank will be the <u>opposite</u> of the word *kind* (such as *unpleasant, unfriendly, cruel*).

Although always kind to strangers, Jennifer is *seldom* _____ to her friends.

The word *seldom* now requires you to choose a word with the <u>same</u> meaning as *kind* (*sympathetic, generous, pleasant, nice*).

Tactics

1. Read the text carefully to get an overall meaning of the passage. If possible, simplify the text in your mind so that you understand the main idea of the text. Try to guess a word or words that could logically complete the text.
2. Pay attention to key function and content words, and watch for "reversers."
3. Don't fill in any blanks until you have read the complete sentence.
4. Examine all possible answers. Look for the words that you guessed that might be possible answers or synonyms of those words. Again, it may be useful to decide if words are generally positive, negative, or neutral. Remember: You don't have to fill the first blank first. It is often easier to fill the second or third blank.
5. Check your answers. Make sure that your choices create a logical sentence. If one of your choices does not make sense, look at the other options.

Example

Stephanie Dexter's European travel guides provide readers with helpful (i) _____ about cozy, family-run hotels. She also offers suggestions about (ii) _____ corporate hotels that they should try to avoid.

Blank (i)	Blank (ii)
(A) warnings	(D) economical
(B) hints	(E) charming
(C) selections	(F) bland

As is often the case, it is easier to solve this problem by finding a possible answer to fill the second blank. Because these hotels should be avoided, a negative adjective is indicated. You could therefore eliminate choice (D), *economical*, and (E), *charming*, which have positive meanings. Choice (F), *bland*, is the best choice; *bland* in this context means "uninteresting." Then look at the first blank. Because the word in the blank is about cozy, family-run hotels, the term *warnings* in (A) is not appropriate; *warnings* are suggestions that something bad is going to happen. Choice (C), *selections*, doesn't really make sense in the context of the sentence. The best choice is (B), *hints* (which means "suggestions").

Again, the items in the Text Completion drills tend to get progressively more difficult, and most here are easier to answer than those on the actual exam.

Text Completion Drill 1

Select **ONE** entry for each column to fill in the corresponding blanks in a way that provides the best completion for the text.

1. The (i) _____ letter could not be published because the newspaper does not print unsigned letters, and it could not be returned because the author had not given his (ii) _____ .

Blank (i)	Blank (ii)
(A) anonymous	(D) opinion
(B) illegible	(E) affiliation
(C) mysterious	(F) address

2. We often think there is _____ between passion and reason, yet the English poet John Donne was able to blend them in his poetry.

(A) a correlation
(B) a disparity
(C) a fusion
(D) an interaction
(E) a transference

3. Almost no diamonds are perfect. Most have (i) _____, some of which (ii)_____ the value of the stone. These "inclusions," as they are called, may make the diamond less (iii) _____ because they interfere with the light as it passes through the stone.

Blank (i)	Blank (ii)	Blank (iii)
(A) flaws	(D) attest to	(G) vulnerable
(B) enhancements	(E) delete	(H) resistant
(C) tints	(F) detract from	(I) brilliant

4. Despite the (i) _____ effort involved in quitting smoking, doctors insist that it is (ii) _____ both in the short-term and the long-term.

Blank (i)	Blank (ii)
(A) prohibitive	(D) innocuous
(B) arduous	(E) beneficial
(C) perennial	(F) distressing

5. Most automobile insurance companies offer discounts to good drivers and charge more to _____ drivers who have poor driving records.

(A) helpless
(B) carefree
(C) fledgling
(D) safety-minded
(E) accident-prone

6. Once hunted almost to extinction because of its beautiful white plumage, the snowy egret is now protected under the Migratory Bird Treaty Act, and its population has _____ .

(A) rebounded
(B) desisted
(C) revolved
(D) descended
(E) emerged

7. The gamelan music of Bali is known for its rapid changes of (i) _____, while Javanese gamelan music tends to be slower and more (ii) _____.

Blank (i)	Blank (ii)
(A) melody	(D) exotic
(B) tempo	(E) intuitive
(C) style	(F) meditative

8. Stendhal's Syndrome, named for the nineteenth-century French novelist who himself fell victim to this disorder, is a psychological condition that causes rapid heartbeat as well as dizziness, confusion, and other feelings of (i) _____. It typically occurs when an individual is exposed to art, especially when the art is particularly "beautiful" or when there is a vast amount of art concentrated in a single place, such as in Florence, Italy, where quite a few cases have been reported. The term is also sometimes used to describe (ii) _____ when one is confronted with a (iii) _____ of sublime beauty in other circumstances, such as when viewing the wonders of the natural world.

Blank (i)	Blank (ii)	Blank (iii)
(A) stimulation	(D) a physical sensation	(G) plethora
(B) inadequacy	(E) a similar reaction	(H) lack
(C) disorientation	(F) an unwelcome response	(I) range

9. No group of animals faces a more urgent need for (i) _____ than do bats. Bats might seem successful, for they are found from the tropics to the Arctic Circle. Moreover, the 977 bat species represent nearly a quarter of all mammalian species. But worldwide, the number of bats is (ii) _____. It is becoming clear that many species of bats, even at the best of times, live very close to their physiological and ecological limits, and even (iii) _____ may push them into extinction.

Blank (i)	Blank (ii)	Blank (iii)
(A) observation	(D) plunging	(G) a slight mishap
(B) protection	(E) stabilizing	(H) an unknown factor
(C) documentation	(F) unknown	(I) a complete disaster

10. Umm Kulthum is widely regarded as the greatest female singer in Arab musical history. The (i) _____ of Umm Kulthum's songs in performance was not (ii)_____ but varied based on the level of emotional interaction between the singer and her audience and Umm Kulthum's own mood. They are nothing short of (iii) _____ in scale, with pieces measured in hours rather than minutes. A typical Umm Kulthum concert consisted of the performance of two or three songs over a period of three to four hours.

Blank (i)	Blank (ii)	Blank (iii)
(A) intensity	(D) fixed	(G) ephemeral
(B) variety	(E) unpredictable	(H) epic
(C) duration	(F) monitored	(I) whimsical

11. Napoleon once said that the characteristic that he (i) _____ most in his generals was luck. While he believed in the importance of strategic planning, he also knew that battles are often tilted one way or another by (ii) _____ series of events that favors one side over another.

Blank (i)	Blank (ii)
(A) overlooked	(D) an unforeseen
(B) prized	(E) an unfortunate
(C) despised	(F) a predictable

12. The B vitamins are eight water-soluble vitamins that work in (i) _____ to boost metabolism, enhance the immune system and nervous system, keep the skin and muscles healthy, encourage cell growth and division, and provide other benefits to the body. (ii) _____, the B vitamins were believed to be a single vitamin, referred to as vitamin B (as today people refer to vitamin C or vitamin D). Later research showed that they are chemically (iii) _____ vitamins that often coexist in the same foods.

Blank (i)	Blank (ii)	Blank (iii)
(A) part	(D) Naturally	(G) inert
(B) tandem	(E) Generally	(H) essential
(C) theory	(F) Historically	(I) discrete

Text Completion Drill 2

Select **ONE** entry from each column to fill in the corresponding blanks in a way that provides the best completion for the text.

1. Despite his impressive education and his reputation as a major poet, John Milton was, in his old age, nearly (i) _____, and he had to depend on the (ii) _____ of his wealthy friends.

Blank (i)	Blank (ii)
(A) successful	(D) knowledge
(B) fashionable	(E) support
(C) indigent	(F) memory

2. A recent study indicates that many surgical procedures are performed (i) _____ and sometimes unnecessarily, and that a policy of "watch and wait" often saves money and (ii) _____ the need for painful operations.

Blank (i)	Blank (ii)
(A) prematurely	(D) buttresses
(B) skillfully	(E) hastens
(C) reluctantly	(F) precludes

3. Senator Collins has (i) _____ style of debating. He often brings up points that are not (ii) _____ to the issues that are being discussed and sometime launches into long digressions about his childhood and his early career. Nevertheless, other candidates find him (iii) _____ opponent.

Blank (i)	Blank (ii)	Blank (iii)
(A) a traditional	(D) germane	(G) a formidable
(B) an aggressive	(E) parallel	(H) an honorable
(C) an unorthodox	(F) comparable	(I) a hesitant

4. Life can be (i) _____, and not just for humans. A recent scientific study by neuroscientist Jaak Panksepp suggests that apes, dogs, and even rats love a good laugh. When chimpanzees play and chase each other, they pant in a manner that is strikingly like human laughter. Panksepp found that rats chirp when they are tickled playfully, in a way that resembles our (ii) _____, and bond socially with their human tickler. And they seem to like it, seeking to be tickled more. Apparently, joyful rats also prefer to hang out with other rats who (iii) _____.

Blank (i)	Blank (ii)	Blank (iii)
(A) challenging	(D) grins	(G) tickle
(B) rewarding	(E) giggles	(H) pant
(C) humorous	(F) sighs	(I) chirp

5. The idea of creating a chess-playing machine dates back to the eighteenth century. Around 1769, the chess-playing automaton called the Chess Turk was built. This machine became famous before it was proved to be (i) _____, when it was discovered that a midget chess player had been hidden inside the mechanism. The field of mechanical chess research (ii) _____ until the advent of the digital computer in the 1950s. Since then, chess enthusiasts and computer engineers have developed chess-playing software with increasing degrees of (iii) _____. Today, free chess apps can be downloaded from the Internet that are challenging even for grand masters.

Blank (i)	Blank (ii)	Blank (iii)
(A) a clever hoax	(D) rebounded	(G) simplicity
(B) an engineering triumph	(E) flourished	(H) sophistication
(C) a disappointing development	(F) languished	(I) comprehension

6. The principle of symmetry has long been an important consideration to artists, artisans, and (i) _____. Indeed, there are few examples of major structural works that do not in some way incorporate the principle of symmetry into their design. Temples, gateways, palaces, and even, in a few cases, entire cities have been created with symmetry as their (ii) _____.

Blank (i)	Blank (ii)
(A) philosophers	(D) guiding tenet
(B) architects	(E) final outcome
(C) rulers	(F) long-term goal

7. It is clear from the letters written by the explorer and map-maker Amerigo Vespucci that he, like Columbus, at first (i) _____ believed that he had reached the wondrous shores of Asia. His writings seemed to (ii) _____ the fantastic accounts that Jehan de Mandeville had written about Asia nearly 200 years earlier. However, by the time of his expedition to South America in 1501, Vespucci was convinced that what he saw was an entirely new landmass, not known to the ancient Greeks; therefore, he (iii) _____ it the "New World."

Blank (i)	Blank (ii)	Blank (iii)
(A) supposedly	(D) gainsay	(G) dubbed
(B) mistakenly	(E) explain	(H) ascertained
(C) defiantly	(F) confirm	(I) discerned

8. People seldom realize that being severely underweight can be equally as danger-ous as being severely overweight, yet this is exactly what a recent study by the Center for Communicative Diseases indicated. (i)_____, the study showed that being slightly overweight actually decreases your chances of dying from non-cancer, non-cardiovascular disease causes of death. But don't start (ii) _____ just yet. People who are even a little overweight have a higher chance of dying from diabetes or kidney disease. Your best bet, of course, is to have a BMI (body mass index) in the normal range.

Blank (i)	Blank (ii)
(A) Theoretically	(D) panicking
(B) In fact	(E) eating donuts
(C) On the contrary	(F) dieting

9. The mathematician James Clerk Maxwell first (i) _____ that light is part of the electro-magnetic spectrum as early as 1864. His equations showed that the patterns and speed of electro-magnetic waves matched the measured pat-terns and speed of light, and he therefore concluded that light itself is indeed part of the electro-magnetic spectrum. Although it took more than twenty years to prove this hypothesis, Heinrich Hertz subsequently designed and built (ii) _____ to physically test this hypothesis and demonstrate that Max-well's theory had been (iii) _____.

Blank (i)	Blank (ii)	Blank (iii)
(A) theorized	(D) an equation	(G) forgotten
(B) determined	(E) an apparatus	(H) incomplete
(C) denied	(F) an assumption	(I) correct

10. When building a robot with two or more legs, one big question is, "How should the robot's brain (i) _____ its legs?" The number of possible gaits (patterns of walking) for a creature with four or more legs is (ii) _____ . Robert McGee of Ohio State University developed a mathematical formula to determine that number. According to that formula, a four-legged walker has more than 5,000 possible gaits, while a six-legged creature has almost 40 million possible ways to walk.

Blank (i)	Blank (ii)
(A) position	(D) limited
(B) extend	(E) specified
(C) coordinate	(F) astronomical

11. During World War II, the U.S. Army employed a number of Navajo Indians as communication specialists. They used a code based on their (i) _____ , and because few if any of the intelligence agents on the other side could comprehend Navajo, these "codetalkers," as they called themselves, could communicate on the radio with no danger that their messages would be (ii) _____ even if they were intercepted. Because there were no words for some military terms in the Navajo language, the code talkers had to substitute (iii) _____ words in place of these terms. For example, for the word *grenade*, they used the Navajo word for "potato," and for *bomber*, they used the Navajo word meaning "eagle."

Blank (i)	Blank (ii)	Blank (iii)
(A) own experiences	(D) misunderstood	(G) invented
(B) native language	(E) deciphered	(H) familiar
(C) intensive training	(F) translated	(I) compound

12. Long before the Aztecs came to the Valley of Mexico, the region had seen the rise and decline of a number of other important groups. One group built the great city of Teotihuacán around 400 A.D. Centuries later another empire was created there by the people known as the Toltecs. Despite the rise and fall of empires, there was a (i) _____ of culture in the Valley of Mexico. Agriculture and other technologies were passed down from generation to generation, as were (ii) _____ concepts: the gods and rituals of one group were inherited by their successors. The pyramidal temples of Teotihuacán were (iii) _____ by the Aztecs seven centuries after the demise of the Teotihuacán Empire.

Blank (i)	Blank (ii)	Blank (iii)
(A) clash	(D) religious	(G) forgotten and abandoned
(B) rearrangement	(E) political	(H) shattered and destroyed
(C) continuity	(F) philosophical	(I) utilized and honored

Text Completion Drill 3

Select **ONE** entry from each column to fill in the corresponding blanks in a way that provides the best completion for the text.

1. Compared to that of animals, the fossil record of plants is quite _____, because plants decay faster than animals given the same initial conditions and because they do not typically have hard parts such as bones that readily fossilize.

(A) sketchy
(B) diversified
(C) confusing
(D) irregular
(E) delicate

2. Artists Christo and his wife Jeanne-Claude's (i) _____ outdoor installations include "Surrounded Islands" and "Wrapped Coast." The former consists of eleven islands in Miami's Biscayne Bay which they surrounded with over half a million square meters of pink plastic, and the latter involved 2.5 kilometers of Australian shoreline which they draped in colorful fabric. Like most of their installations, these works of environmental art initially faced resistance and (ii) _____ from the authorities and the public alike, but eventually they were accepted and admired.

Blank (i)	Blank (ii)
(A) colossal	(D) tolerance
(B) lucrative	(E) deception
(C) symbolic	(F) skepticism

3. Scientist and author Rachel Carson's book *Silent Spring* sparked (i) _____ at the time of its publication. In it, she detailed how the uncontrolled and irresponsible use of pesticides such as DDT poison the food supply of animals, kill birds and fish, and contaminate human food. Spokespersons for the chemical industry (ii) _____ personal attacks against Carson and issued propaganda to prove that her findings were flawed. However, her work was (iii) _____ by a 1963 report of President Kennedy's Science Advisory Committee.

Blank (i)	Blank (ii)	Blank (iii)
(A) intense introspection	(D) resented	(G) instigated
(B) heated controversy	(E) forestalled	(H) inspired
(C) utter misconception	(F) fomented	(I) vindicated

4. Wild rabbits are _____ creatures that mainly rely on their acute sense of hearing to warn them of danger and their speed to flee from predators.

(A) vigorous
(B) graceful
(C) aggressive
(D) unpredictable
(E) timid

5. Built on a hill in Philadelphia in 1839, the imposing, castle-like structure known as Eastern State Penitentiary was once the largest building in the United States. At the time it was built, the (i) _____ theory of penology was based on principles of the Quaker religion. It was thought that if prisoners reflected in (ii) _____ on the wrongs they had committed, they would be reformed. Therefore, inmates ate alone, slept alone, and worked at crafts such as furniture-making or basket-weaving alone in their cells. They even had (iii) _____ areas outside their cells where they could exercise and breathe fresh air for an hour a day, unobserved by other prisoners.

Blank (i)	Blank (ii)	Blank (iii)
(A) austere	(D) introspective solitude	(G) sumptuous
(B) prevailing	(E) silent abandonment	(H) secluded
(C) essential	(F) blatant indifference	(I) deserted

6. Few shoppers put candy bars, chewing gum, and celebrity magazines on their lists when they go to the supermarket, but as they wait in check-out lines they may purchase these items on a sudden (i) _____. A recent study showed that impulse buying dropped by about 25% when shoppers used self-check-out lines and scanned their own purchases. Researchers theorized that there are two reasons for this. For one thing, shoppers who choose the self-check-out option usually spend less time waiting in line. For another, there are generally fewer snacks and other (ii) _____ impulse items in the vicinity of these scanners.

Blank (i)	Blank (ii)
(A) whim	(D) convenient
(B) requirement	(E) tempting
(C) sensation	(F) banal

7. In an unusual decision, Marie Curie and her husband intentionally (i) _____ from patenting the radium-isolation process that they had developed so that the scientific community could continue the Curies' research (ii) _____.

Blank (i)	Blank (ii)
(A) recovered	(D) unopposed
(B) detached	(E) unspecified
(C) refrained	(F) unhampered

8. The existence of the Higgs boson particle, which is thought to be key to our understanding of the structure of matter, was first proposed back in 1964. Scientists have spent decades seeking proof that it exists, but only in recent years, by using the Large Hadron Supercollider, have they begun to close in on this _____ particle.

| (A) negligible |
| (B) quaint |
| (C) sly |
| (D) elusive |
| (E) intensive |

9. In early games of basketball, the "basket" was literally a basket; two peach baskets were nailed to the walls at either end of the court. In contrast to modern basketball nets, the peach baskets (i) _____ their bottoms, and balls had to be (ii) _____ manually after each successful shot.

Blank (i)	Blank (ii)
(A) secured	(D) retrieved
(B) retained	(E) deconstructed
(C) plugged	(F) recalled

10. Vance Packard's 1957 book, *The Hidden Persuaders*, deals with the (i) _____ tactics used by advertisers to (ii) _____ consumers to buy products whether they need them or not by using the techniques of applied psychology and sociology. The book goes on to question the morality of using these methods to create a demand for products and services.

Blank (i)	Blank (ii)
(A) genuine	(D) apprise
(B) enchanting	(E) cope with
(C) sinister	(F) allure

11. Possibly the earliest use of diamonds was for polishing axes. According to evidence found by Harvard physicist Peter Lu, the ancient Chinese used diamonds to _____ their ceremonial axes. These ceremonial weapons were made of corundum, the second-hardest naturally occurring substance on earth. Only the hardest substance, diamonds, could be used to bring them to a mirror finish.

(A) sharpen
(B) forge
(C) tarnish
(D) buttress
(E) burnish

12. Robert Bernasconi has tackled the Promethean task of (i)_____ the writings of Jean-Paul Sartre, one of the most prolific of the great philoso   phers of the 20th century, into under a hundred pages. Bernasconi, a widely recognized expert in existential philosophy, seems acutely aware that Sartre's prose is (ii)_____ and opaque, and that the task of conveying his thought from a limited selection of extracts is (iii) _____ one.

Blank (i)	Blank (ii)	Blank (iii)
(A) condensing	(D) tortuous	(G) a comprehensive
(B) revising	(E) brilliant	(H) a magnificent
(C) describing	(F) pellucid	(I) an arduous

Text Completion Drill 4

Select **one** entry from each column to fill in the corresponding blanks in a way that provides the best completion for the text.

1. Despite his reputation as _____ and intractable negotiator, the labor leader seemed to be in a conciliatory mood at the first meeting.

(A) an inventive
(B) a truculent
(C) an inconsistent
(D) an irresolute
(E) a halfhearted

2. Large brass statues which were mass-produced in plaster. At the height of their popularity, his figurines could be seen in the parlors of many homes across the United States.

(A) replicas of
(B) sketches of
(C) features of
(D) additions to
(E) accessories for

3. The main difference between table salt and coarse salt lies in their (i) _____. Table salt is smooth and is made up of very (ii) _____ particles. However, coarse salt is composed of large, crystalline grains, and therefore is also called rock salt.

Blank (i)	Blank (ii)
(A) taste	(D) sharp
(B) chemistry	(E) fine
(C) texture	(F) light-weight

4. Dolley Madison became first lady of the United States in 1809. Her _____ personality contrasted sharply with the shy and stone-faced disposition of her husband, President James Madison.

| (A) impassive |
| (B) vivacious |
| (C) insipid |
| (D) cynical |
| (E) domineering |

5. It is generally understood that a ballad is a song that tells a story, but a folk song is not so easily _____.

| (A) composed |
| (B) appreciated |
| (C) endorsed |
| (D) defined |
| (E) concluded |

6. Snails are most often seen on _____ days because direct sunlight can dry out and damage their skin.

| (A) summer |
| (B) humid |
| (C) overcast |
| (D) brilliant |
| (E) short |

7. From 1945 until about 1970, the colonial empires of Britain, France, and other European powers (i) _____ as, one after another, their former overseas possessions became (ii) _____ .

Blank (i)	Blank (ii)
(A) reorganized	(D) autonomous
(B) crumbled	(E) disenfranchised
(C) flourished	(F) alienated

8. The vuvuzela, a plastic horn that produces a loud, monotone note, has become the symbol of South African football, filling stadiums with a raucous (i) _____ . The vuvuzela became the subject of controversy at the 2010 World Cup games. Competitors complained that the noise (ii) _____ communication among players, and broadcasters insisted that commentators' voices were being (iii) _____ by the noise.

Blank (i)	Blank (ii)	Blank (iii)
(A) cacophony	(D) insured	(G) held up
(B) competition	(E) hindered	(H) drowned out
(C) virulence	(F) necessitated	(I) forced down

9. During the snow drought of the 1970s, the U. S. government (i) _____ organized a cloud-seeding program in the western states. The success of this crash program was difficult to (ii) _____ , however, because it is impossible to know for certain how much (iii) _____ would have fallen without these weather modification projects.

Blank (i)	Blank (ii)	Blank (iii)
(A) convincingly	(D) gauge	(G) temperatures
(B) reportedly	(E) believe	(H) expectations
(C) hastily	(F) deny	(I) precipitation

10. Dressage, called by some people "horse ballet," is perhaps the ultimate test of communication between horse and rider. To (i) _____, there seems to be no interaction at all between riders and their mounts, but in fact, there is a con stant stream of almost (ii) _____ commands.

Blank (i)	Blank (ii)
(A) the expert participant	(D) indeterminate
(B) the untrained eye	(E) imperceptible
(C) an official judge	(F) unintelligible

11. Snow leopards show several (i) _____ to life in a cold, mountainous environment. Their bodies are stocky, their fur is thick, and their ears are small and rounded, all of which help to (ii) _____ heat loss. The snow leopard also has large nasal cavities that help the animals breathe the thin, cold, alpine air.

Blank (i)	Blank (ii)
(A) adaptations	(D) conserve
(B) inclinations	(E) stimulate
(C) aspirations	(F) minimize

12. James Boswell is best known for his biography of the British literary figure Samuel Johnson. His (i) _____ has passed into the English language as a term for a constant companion and observer, especially one who records those observations in print. In one of the short stories about Sherlock Holmes, the fictional detective Holmes affectionately says of Dr. Watson, who dutifully (ii) _____ all the cases that Holmes solves, "I am lost without my Boswell."

Blank (i)	Blank (ii)
(A) nickname	(D) documents
(B) reputation	(E) critiques
(C) surname	(F) interprets

Text Completion Drill 5

Select **ONE** entry from each column to fill in the corresponding blanks in a way that provides the best completion for the text.

1. The flag of Nepal is _____ in that it is the only official national flag that is not rectangular in shape.

(A) autonomous
(B) redundant
(C) controversial
(D) unique
(E) divisive

2. Although Mr. Porter has a history of making (i) _____ investments, his latest financial venture has been a (ii) _____ success.

Blank (i)	Blank (ii)
(A) thoughtful	(D) problematic
(B) shrewd	(E) resounding
(C) rash	(F) partial

3. In 1947, poet W. H. Auden wrote the book *The Age of Anxiety*, in which he (i) _____ the problems and fears of ordinary people such as shop clerks and bank tellers. Since then, the phrase "age of anxiety" has come to denote any time marked by (ii) _____ and danger.

Blank (i)	Blank(ii)
(A) celebrates	(D) intransigence
(B) delineates	(E) turmoil
(C) embellishes	(F) equanimity

4. First introduced in the 1970s, ATMs (i) _____ madly during the 1980s and 90s, and today they are (ii)_____.

Blank (i)	Blank (ii)
(A) inundated	(D) populous
(B) proliferated	(E) infamous
(C) converged	(F) ubiquitous

5. Good handwriting is not necessarily the sign of a strong character, as even a (i) _____ glance at the nearly _____ penmanship of John F. Kennedy, Winston Churchill, Bill Gates, Albert Einstein, or Mahatma Gandhi shows.

Blank (i)	Blank (ii)
(A) cursory	(D) intelligible
(B) desultory	(E) irresolute
(C) assiduous	(F) illegible

6. At the end of every month in which sales figures go down, the sales reps are forced to listen to their sales manager (i) _____ them about their lack of (ii) _____in signing new accounts.

Blank (i)	Blank (ii)
(A) harangue	(D) resistance
(B) apprise	(E) initiative
(C) laud	(F) chicanery

7. In comparison to the band's earlier releases, which were all (i) _____, crowd-pleasing pop songs, some of the songs on their new CD are as solemn and slow as (ii) _____.

Blank (i)	Blank (ii)
(A) unorthodox	(D) anthems
(B) morose	(E) dirges
(C) upbeat	(F) codas

8. Devising a (i) _____ but incredibly time-consuming style called Pointillism, the Post-Impressionist painter Georges Seurat (ii) _____ broad brushstrokes of mixed color with tiny points of pure color which the observer's eye reconstructs as comprehensible images in much the same way that the eye (iii) _____ bits of light into images.

Blank (i)	Blank (ii)	Blank (iii)
(A) backbreaking	(D) replaced	(G) shatters
(B) groundbreaking	(E) focused	(H) assembles
(C) foot dragging	(F) inserted	(I) defines

9. After a period of about twenty minutes of being exposed to a strong smell, the odor receptors in our noses become (i) _____ and stop sending messages to the brain. This happens whether we are smelling the sweet fragrance of roses or the appetizing scent of bread baking. Mercifully, our noses also become (ii) _____ to the scent of (iii) _____ odors such as those of spoiled fish or rotten eggs.

Blank (i)	Blank (ii)	Blank (iii)
(A) desensitized	(D) simulated	(G) insipid
(B) repulsed	(E) inured	(H) sumptuous
(C) convoluted	(F) enervated	(I) noisome

10. Despite their (i) _____, it turns out that tomato growers are to blame for tasteless tomatoes. By breeding tomatoes that ripen evenly, harvest easily, and have a uniform red color, they inadvertently robbed those sumptuous fruit of their flavor. University of California biochemist Ann Powell has (ii) _____ the exact genetic mutation responsible for the loss of sweetness. What makes tomatoes attractive and easy to grow is a disabled GLK2 gene, and the (iii) _____ of this is a tomato that tastes like soggy cardboard.

Blank (i)	Blank (ii)	Blank (iii)
(A) meticulous planning	(D) synthesized	(G) unwelcome consequence
(B) explicit directions	(E) pinpointed	(H) fortuitousoutcome
(C) best intentions	(F) formulated	(I) unintended cause

11. Scientists sometimes struggle to communicate their knowledge to non-scientists because they find it difficult to simplify their ideas sufficiently for theiraudience to comprehend them. Furthermore, many scientists have not been trained to be good communicators. However, astrophysicist Neil deGrasse Tyson's (i) _____ style of delivery and his ability to explain even the most (ii)_____ theories in ways that everyone can understand make him extremely popular with a wide audience and a higly-desirable talk-show guest.

Blank (i)	Blank (ii)
(A) pedantic	(D) recondite
(B) bombastic	(E) comprehensible
(C) affable	(F) inconsequential

12. The golden tortoise beetle can alter its color within a short time period, turning from a (i) _____ metallic gold color to a dull, spotty reddish color in order to conceal itself. The insect has a thin layer of liquid beneath its trans parent outer layer of chitin which it can (ii) _____ when it needs to, changing the thickness of the layer of liquid, and thus changing its color and reflectivity. This change of color also occurs (iii) _____ when the beetle is under moisture-stress.

Blank (i)	Blank (ii)	Blank (iii)
(A) luminous	(D) inflict	(G) profoundly
(B) inert	(E) compress	(H) freely
(C) pungent	(F) refine	(I) involuntarily

4 Vocabulary Building

360 Common GRE Words

These words have appeared or are likely to appear in Sentence Equivalence and Text Completion items. Following this list are examples of how these words are used. You'll need to identify the part of speech (noun, verb, adjective, etc.) and provide brief definitions or synonyms for the word. After each set of 15 words, there is an exercise that will help you become more familiar with this vocabulary.

Set 1

1. abate
2. aberrant
3. (in) abeyance
4. abscond
5. abstain
6. abstruse
7. abysmal
8. acerbic
9. acrid
10. acrimonious
11. adamant
12. admonish
13. affable
14. alacrity
15. alleviate

Set 2

16. allure
17. aloof
18. ambiguous
19. ameliorate
20. amiable
21. antipathy
22. apathetic
23. appease
24. apprise
25. approbation
26. apt
27. arbitrary
28. archaic
29. ardent
30. arduous

Set 3

31. arid
32. assiduous
33. astute
34. audacious
35. auspicious
36. austere
37. avert
38. baffling
39. banal
40. belie
41. beneficent
42. berate
43. bicker
44. bland
45. bolster (v.)

Set 4

46. bombastic
47. boorish
48. burgeon
49. burnish
50. buttress (v.)
51. cacophonous
52. candid
53. canny
54. capricious
55. castigate
56. caustic
57. charismatic
58. cherish
59. chicanery
60. clandestine

Set 5

61. cogent
62. colossal
63. complacent
64. complaisant
65. comply
66. congenial
67. congested
68. conflate
69. conspicuous
70. contentious
71. contraption
72. conundrum
73. converge
74. convoluted
75. copious

Set 6

76. cordial
77. covert
78. craven
79. curb (v.)
80. cursory
81. daunt
82. dearth
83. deference
84. denigrate
85. deplete
86. deplorable
87. desiccate
88. destitute
89. desultory
90. diatribe

Set 7

91. diffident
92. diffuse
93. digress
94. diligent
95. disabuse
96. discern
97. discredit
98. discreet
99. discrete
100. disingenuous
101. disinterested
102. disjointed
103. disparage
104. disparate
105. dissemble

Set 8

106. disseminate
107. divert
108. drench
109. dwindle
110. ebullient
111. eccentric
112. eclectic
113. elusive
114. empirical
115. emulate
116. enervate
117. engender
118. enigma
119. ephemeral
120. erudite

Set 9

121. esoteric
122. exacerbate
123. exculpate
124. execrable
125. exigency
126. exotic
127. facetious
128. fallow
129. fastidious
130. fatuous
131. feasible
132. feckless
133. felicitous
134. ervent
135. flamboyant

Set 10

136. flaunt
137. fledgling
138. fleeting
139. flout
140. fluke
141. foolhardy
142. forestall
143. formidable
144. frivolity
145. frugal
146. garrulous
147. gaudy
148. gauge (v.)
149. germane
150. gregarious

Set 11

151. gullible
152. hamper (v.)
153. haphazard
154. harangue
155. hasty
156. hazardous
157. hegemony
158. hiatus
159. hinder
160. hoax
161. humdrum
162. impassive
163. impecunious
164. imperious
165. impervious

Set 12

166. importune
167. impromptu
168. impulsive
169. inadvertent
170. inchoate
171. incisive
172. incongruous
173. indigent
174. indifferent
175. inept
176. infamous
177. ingenious
178. insinuate
179. insipid
180. insular

Set 13

181. intrepid
182. invaluable
183. invigorate
184. itinerant
185. jargon
186. juxtapose
187. knack
188. lackadaisical
189. laconic
190. lamentable
191. languish
192. lassitude
193. lax
194. lenient
195. lethargic

Set 14

196. levity
197. lionize
198. loquacious
199. lucid
200. lucrative
201. ludicrous
202. lugubrious
203. luminous
204. malodorous
205. mar
206. meander
207. mediocre
208. mendacious
209. mercurial
210. meticulous

Set 15

211. minute (adj.)
212. miserly
213. mitigate
214. mollify
215. mordant
216. moribund
217. morose
218. mundane
219. mushroom (v.)
220. myriad
221. mythical
222. neophyte
223. noisome
224. nonchalant
225. nostalgic

Set 16

226. notorious
227. obdurate
228. oblivious
229. obtuse
230. obviate
231. officious
232. onerous
233. orthodox
234. ostentatious
235. oversee
236. overt
237. pacify
238. paucity
239. pedestrian (adj.)
240. palpable

Set 17

241. parched
242. pensive
243. penurious
244. perfunctory
245. perilous
246. peripheral
247. petulant
248. pithy
249. pivotal
250. placate
251. plethora
252. plight
253. plummet
254. plunge
255. plush

Set 18

256. precarious
257. preclude
258. preposterous
259. prescient
260. prevaricate
261. pristine
262. prodigious
263. profligate
264. prolific
265. prolix
266. propitious
267. prosaic
268. puerile
269. pungent
270. quaint

Set 19

271. qualm
272. quandary
273. querulous
274. quibble
275. quiescent
276. quirk
277. quotidian
278. rapacious
279. rash (adj.)
280. raucous
281. rebound
282. recalcitrant
283. recondite
284. relish (v.)
285. restive

Set 20

286. reticent
287. rustic
288. sage (adj.)
289. salubrious
290. sanguine
291. savvy
292. scathing
293. scrutinize
294. sedulous
295. shard
296. shrewd
297. simulate
298. sketchy
299. solicitous
300. somber

Set 21

301. sonorous
302. soporific
303. specious
304. sporadic
305. spurious
306. spurn
307. squabble
308. squander
309. stimulate
310. subtle
311. sumptuous
312. taciturn
313. (in) tandem
314. tangential
315. tangible

Set 22

316. tarnish
317. tenet
318. tenuous
319. tepid
320. terse
321. thrifty
322. thwart
323. tirade
324. topple
325. torpor
326. tortuous
327. transitory
328. trenchant
329. trite
330. truculent

Set 23

331. turbulent
332. tyro
333. ubiquitous
334. uncouth
335. unsullied
336. upbraid
337. urbane
338. vacillate
339. vapid
340. veracious
341. verbose
342. versatile
343. vex
344. vie
345. vindicate

Set 24

346. viscous
347. vituperative
348. vivacious
349. voracious
350. wane
351. wary
352. waver
353. whimsical
354. wince
355. wishy-washy
356. wistful
357. woe
358. woo
359. wretched
360. zealous

Directions:

For each vocabulary item, first read the context sentence and try to guess the meaning of the target word. Then look up the word using a web-based dictionary such as dictionary.com, thesaurus.com, or merriam-webster.com. You can also use a monolingual paper-based dictionary. Give the part of speech (noun, verb, adj) and one or more synonyms or definitions.

Notice that, for some entries, related forms are also given (for example, for the verb *abate*, the negative –*ed* adjective *unabated* is given). These are not a complete list of related forms, only ones that might appear on the test.

Vocabulary Set 1: (*abate* to *alleviate*)

1. **abate** The trend for restaurants to serve locally-produced foods shows no sign of <u>abating</u>.
part of speech <u>**verb**</u> definition/synonyms <u>*lessen, weaken, decrease*</u>
neg. –ed adj: **unabated**

2. **aberrant** I studied <u>aberrant</u> behavior in my abnormal psychology class.
part of speech _____ definition/synonyms _____

3. (in) **abeyance** At one time, it was possible to have small savings accounts at local U.S. Post Offices, but that program has been in <u>abeyance</u> for decades.
part of speech _____ definition/synonyms _____

4. **abscond** The police are looking for an employee of the jewelry store who <u>absconded</u> with a briefcase full of diamond jewelry.
part of speech _____ definition/synonyms _____

5. **abstain** Vegans <u>abstain</u> from eating meat or any animal products such as milk or eggs.
part of speech _____ definition/synonyms _____
noun: **abstention**

6. **acerbic** Stephanie always seems pleasant to the other students in her study group, but when they are not around, she sometimes makes <u>acerbic</u> comments about them
part of speech _____ definition/synonyms _____

7. **abstruse** The articles in the journal *Modern Math* are just too <u>abstruse</u> for most people without advanced degrees in mathematics to understand.
part of speech _____ definition/synonyms _____

8. **abysmal** Our team's record so far this year has been <u>abysmal</u>. We've lost every game but one.
part of speech _____ definition/synonyms _____
adv: **abysmally**

9. **acrid** Somehow, that huge pile of used tires caught on fire. The burning rubber produced an <u>acrid</u> smell.
part of speech _____ definition/synonyms _____

10. **acrimonious** When they were at the university, Greg and Kevin were close friends, but afterwards, their relationship turned <u>acrimonious</u>.
part of speech _____ definition/synonyms _____

11. **adamant** Her professor suggested Mei change the topic of her thesis slightly, but she was <u>adamant</u> in her refusal.
part of speech _____ definition/synonyms _____
adv: **adamantly**

12. **admonish** The police officer <u>admonished</u> the driver for speeding through a school zone.
part of speech _____ definition/synonyms _____

13. **affable** Our <u>affable</u> host welcomed us to his house and told us to make ourselves at home.
part of speech _____ definition/synonyms _____
adv: **affably**

14. (with) **alacrity** Jim had always wanted to teach, so he accepted the position as Professor Hill's teaching assistant with <u>alacrity</u>.
part of speech _____ definition/synonyms _____

15. **alleviate** Although it rained heavily last night, one single storm will do little to <u>alleviate</u> the drought conditions.
part of speech _____ definition/synonyms _____

Vocabulary Exercise 1: Fill in the Blanks

Fill in the blanks in the sentences below with one of the words from this list to form a logical sentence.

acrid	affable	abate
abstain	adamant	alacrity
aberrant	acerbic	abscond
abeyance	alleviate	admonished
abstruse	abysmal	

1. The dishonest accountant tried to _____ to South America with the money that he had stolen from the company.

2. My new intern is a really good worker. He does all the tasks that I assign to him with _____.

3. The council member couldn't decide whether to vote YES or NO on the measure, so he decided to _____ from voting.

4. Just a few days on the beach seemed to _____ Jan's stress.

5. Eric's behavior has been growing more and more _____. He just isn't acting like himself these days.

6. The high school used to have a drivers' education program, but it is currently in _____.

7. People who live near the paper factory are complaining because it is emitting some _____, sulfurous fumes.

8. After about an hour, the thunderstorm began to _____.

9. The director _____ the actor for missing the rehearsal.

10. Liza has quite an _____ sense of humor. She's funny, but sometimes people are insulted by her jokes.

11. I learned a little about string theory in my physics class, but I still find it an _____ concept. It's puzzling and mysterious to me.

12. Despite an _____ grade on my mid-term exam, I got a B in class because I did well on the final and I got an A- on my research paper.

Vocabulary Set 2: (*allure* to *arduous*)

---

16. allure Meglamart's new commercials are intended to <u>allure</u> customers back to their stores.

part of speech _____ definition/synonyms _____

noun: **allure** -ing adj: **alluring**

---

17. aloof When Keiko was our co-worker, she was warm and friendly, and she often had lunch with us. But since she has been promoted to manager, she acts <u>aloof</u>, and the only time she talks to us is to give orders.

part of speech _____ definition/synonyms _____

---

18. ambiguous I didn't exactly understand what the professor meant when she answered my question. Her response was <u>ambiguous</u>.

part of speech _____ definition/synonyms _____

noun: **ambiguity** adv: **ambiguously**

---

19. ameliorate The city is taking several steps to <u>ameliorate</u> traffic problems.

part of speech _____ definition/synonyms _____

---

20. amiable Although the email began with an <u>amiable</u> greeting, it then took on a hostile tone.

part of speech _____ definition/synonyms _____

adv: **amiably**

---

21. antipathy He may be my competitor, but I feel no <u>antipathy</u> towards him personally.

part of speech _____ definition/synonyms _____

---

22. apathetic Chang doesn't really care who wins tomorrow's game. He's completely <u>apathetic</u> about the outcome.

part of speech _____ definition/synonyms _____

noun: **apathy**

---

23. appease Jenifer was somewhat <u>appeased</u> when her friend apologized for insulting her.

part of speech _____ definition/synonyms _____

noun: **appeasement**

---

24. **apprise** Although there was no cell phone service, the journalist was able to apprise her viewers of the situation by satellite phone.
part of speech _____ definition/synonyms _____

25. **approbation** Sometimes a mayor will award someone a "key to the city" as a sign of approbation. This practice goes back to the time when medieval cities were surrounded by walls and the gates were locked at night. Back then, the key to a city was not just a symbolic award—it actually had a practical use.
part of speech _____ definition/synonyms _____

26. **apt** The song that the band played as the first song at the wedding reception turned out to be an apt choice. It was the couple's favorite song. part of speech _____ definition/synonyms _____
Alejandra is an apt student; she'll probably get an A+.
part of speech _____ definition/synonyms _____
I'm apt to make plenty of mistakes when I speak French; it's been a long time since I took a French course.
part of speech _____ definition/synonyms _____
adv: **aptly**

27. **arbitrary** While the rules of this game may seem arbitrary, they are actually carefully thought out.
part of speech _____ definition/synonyms _____
adv: **arbitrarily**

28. **archaic** The word _prithee_ is considered archaic today. It was used in Shakespearean English to ask a question or make a request. "Aye, prithee, sing" means "Yes, please sing a song."
part of speech _____ definition/synonyms _____

29. **ardent** Rudolfo is an ardent fan of his local football club. He never misses one of their games.
part of speech _____ definition/synonyms _____
noun: **ardor** adv: **ardently**

30. **arduous** An Ironman Triathlon is an incredibly arduous competition. It involves a 2.4-mile (3.9 km.) swim, a 112-mile (180 km.) bicycle ride, and a full 26.2-mile (42.2 km.) marathon run.
part of speech _____ definition/synonyms _____

Vocabulary Exercise 2: Matching

Match these words with their synonyms.

1. approbation ___
2. aloof ___
3. amiable___
4. apprise ___
5. archaic ___
6. antipathy ___
7. arduous ___
8. apathetic ___
9. alluring __
10. ardent ___

A. old-fashioned; not currently in use; antiquated
B. hatred; intense dislike; aversion
C. remote; unfriendly; cold
D. cordial; agreeable; affable; amicable
E. appealing; attractive; tempting
F. to notify; inform; explain
G. approval; praise; commendation
H. eager; enthusiastic; zealous; passionate
I. challenging; difficult; grueling; hard
J. indifferent; unconcerned; uninterested

Vocabulary Set 3: (*arid* to *bolster*)

31. **arid** On the border between Bolivia and Peru is the Atacama Desert, the most <u>arid</u> region in the world. In some parts of the desert, there has been no rainfall at all for hundreds of years.
part of speech _____ definition/synonyms _____
noun: **aridity**

32. **assiduous** One reason Alice was able to get a new job was that her former boss wrote her a glowing letter of recommendation. He said that she was quite an <u>assiduous</u> worker.
part of speech _____ definition/synonyms _____
adv: **assiduously**

33. **astute** Some of the reviews in that magazine are silly, but their review of Alex Healy's new novel is quite <u>astute</u>.
part of speech _____ definition/synonyms _____
adv: **astutely**

34. **audacious** In 1926, Admiral Byrd and pilot Floyd Bennett undertook an <u>audacious</u> mission. They were the first to fly to the North Pole.
part of speech _____ definition/synonyms _____
noun: **audacity**

35. **auspicious** The play had an <u>auspicious</u> first act, but by the middle of the second act, I was starting to get bored.
part of speech _____ definition/synonyms _____
neg. adj: **inauspicious**

36. **austere** Boston City Hall is an example of an <u>austere</u> style of architecture called "Brutalism." The building is extremely plain and lacks all ornamentation.
part of speech _____ definition/synonyms _____
noun: **austerity**

37. **avert** Some "smart" cars have technology that automatically helps drivers <u>avert</u> accidents.
part of speech _____ definition/synonyms _____

38. **baffling** I just finished reading a book about quantum physics. I understood some of the ideas in the book, but others were <u>baffling</u>.
part of speech _____ definition/synonyms _____
verb: **baffle**

39. **banal** Some people want to know everything about their favorite celebrities, including the most <u>banal</u> details.
part of speech _____ definition/synonyms _____
noun: **banality**

40. **belie** Richard claims that he has very little money, but his new Mercedes and his five Armani suits <u>belie</u> that claim.
part of speech _____ definition/synonyms _____

41. **beneficent** <u>Beneficent</u> alumni donated millions to the university last year.
part of speech _____ definition/synonyms _____
noun: **beneficence**

42. **berate** The coach never <u>berated</u> his players when they made mistakes. He simply pointed out ways they could improve their game.
part of speech _____ definition/synonyms _____

43. **bicker** I wish Peter and his sister would stop <u>bickering</u>—all they ever do is argue, argue, argue!
part of speech _____ definition/synonyms _____

44. **bland** Compared to most of the dishes on the menu, this stew is fairly <u>bland</u>.
part of speech _____ definition/synonyms _____

45. **bolster** Taking a few ski lessons <u>bolstered</u> my confidence on the slopes.
part of speech _____ definition/synonyms _____

Vocabulary Exercise 3: Multiple Choice

Choose the word or words that are closest in meaning to the underlined word.

1. Her career got off to an <u>auspicious</u> start.
    A. disappointing   B. promising   C. unusual

2. I found the architect's plan for the new building to be quite <u>bland</u>.
    A. unexciting   B. dynamic   C. unorthodox

3. This article explains some ways to <u>avert</u> a cold or the flu.
    A. shorten   B. cure   C. avoid

4. The girls' father told them to stop <u>bickering</u>.
    A. complaining   B. crying   C. quarrelling

5. Ms. O'Neill's gift was quite <u>beneficent</u>.
    A. unexpected   B. generous   C. welcome

6. The expressions on the faces of the people in this old family photo are quite <u>austere</u>.
    A. affectionate and happy   B. difficult to understand   C. cold and unsmiling

7. The climate in the northern part of this province is quite <u>arid</u>.
    A. dry   B. chilly   C. windy

8. There are several ways you could <u>bolster</u> the arguments in your essay.
    A. explain   B. restate   C. support

9. He <u>berated</u> the quality of these new products.
    A. analyzed   B. criticized   C. promoted

10. They dreamed up quite an <u>audacious</u> plan.
    A. daring   B. clever   C. successful

Vocabulary Set 4: (*bombastic* to *clandestine*)

---

46. **bombastic** I thought all of the candidates who spoke at the rally were <u>bombastic</u>. I prefer to listen to a simple, straightforward speech.

part of speech _____ definition/synonyms _____

noun: **bombast**

---

47. **boorish** Helen was embarrassed by her brother's <u>boorish</u> behavior at the reception.

part of speech _____ definition/synonyms _____

adv: **boorishly** agent noun: **boor***

---

48. **burgeon** Until 1896, Seattle was a tiny frontier outpost, the site of several timber mills. However, with the discovery of gold in Alaska, it <u>burgeoned</u> into a busy transportation hub.

part of speech _____ definition/synonyms _____

-ing adj: **burgeoning**

---

49. **burnish** He <u>burnished</u> the brass buttons on his coat so that they shone in the sun.

part of speech _____ definition/synonyms _____

-ed adj: **burnished**

---

50. **cacophonous** The children were banging on pots and pans and singing off-key, creating quite a <u>cacophonous</u> noise.

part of speech _____ definition/synonyms _____

noun: **cacophony**

---

51. **buttress** Her claim to have seen a UFO was <u>buttressed</u> by a video that a neighbor had made.

part of speech _____ definition/synonyms _____

---

52. **candid** The police suspected that Ms. Martindale was not being completely <u>candid</u> because the story she told them this morning did not match the story she had told them last night.

part of speech _____ definition/synonyms _____

noun: **candor**

53. **canny** He was a <u>canny</u> politician. He had years of experience and knew a lot of tricks.
part of speech _____ definition/synonyms _____

54. **capricious** Alicia can be <u>capricious</u>. A few weeks ago she was planning to do a semester abroad in Paris, then she was going to study in Rio, and now she wants to learn Japanese in Tokyo.
part of speech _____ definition/synonyms _____
noun: **caprice**

55. **castigate** The manager of the restaurant <u>castigated</u> the waiter for being rude to customers.
part of speech _____ definition/synonyms _____
noun: **castigation**

56. **caustic** Joana's feelings were hurt by her boss's <u>caustic</u> remark
part of speech _____ definition/synonyms _____

57. **charismatic** President John F. Kennedy was known for his <u>charismatic</u> style of leadership.
part of speech _____ definition/synonyms _____
noun: **charisma** neg. adj: **uncharismatic**

58. **cherish** Wendy was delighted when someone found the sapphire ring that her father had given her. It was one of her most <u>cherished</u> possessions.
part of speech _____ definition/synonyms _____
-ed adj: **cherished**

59. **chicanery** They set up a false corporation and, through <u>chicanery</u>, they were able to cheat their investors.
part of speech _____ definition/synonyms _____

60. <u>**clandestine**</u> Industrial spies are sometimes hired by corporations to conduct <u>clandestine</u> activities in order to steal secrets from other companies
part of speech _____ definition/synonyms _____

An agent noun is a person or thing that does something or has certain characteristics. For example, the agent noun for write is writer; the agent noun for erase is eraser. In this case, a boor is a boorish person.

Vocabulary Exercise 4: Error Check

If the sentences below are true or logical, mark them **YES**. If the sentences are false or illogical, mark them **NO**.

___ 1. I like to study in <u>cacophonous</u> places, such as the university library.

___ 2. <u>Boorish</u> guests are always welcome at a formal dinner party.

___ 3. If a knight <u>burnishes</u> his shield and his armor, they become shiny and clean.

___ 4. A <u>banal</u> idea is creative and innovative.

___ 5. The words *bolster* and <u>buttress</u> are similar in meaning.

___ 6. The weather here can be quite <u>capricious</u>, especially in the early spring. It may be sunny in the morning, raining in the afternoon, and snowing at night.

___ 7. It was a <u>clandestine</u> meeting. Everyone was invited to attend.

___ 8. The dormitories are all full because the number of students at the university has <u>burgeoned</u> in recent years.

___ 9. He was <u>castigated</u> for being a hero.

___ 10. A few <u>caustic</u> comments are always appreciated.

Crossword Puzzle 1: Sets 1-4 (*abate* to *clandestine*)

Across

1 Trickery; fraud; deception
4 Not willing to change one's mind; stubborn; resolute
6 Unfriendly; cold; distant
8 Flavorless; mild; insipid
11 Noisy; loud and unpleasant
12 Unmannered; rude; impolite; crude
13 Warn; scold; criticize
14 Cheerful willingness; eagerness
16 To attract; tempt; appeal to
17 Secret; hidden; covert

Down

1 Honest; sincere; frank
2 Unconcerned; indifferent; uncaring
3 Confusing; difficult to understand
5 To avoid; prevent
6 Challenging; difficult; onerous
7 Changeable; whimsical; impulsive
9 To run away, especially to avoid capture; flee
10 Intense dislike
12 To argue about minor points; squabble
13 Very dry; parched
15 Having a strong, bitter smell or taste

Vocabulary Set 5: (*cogent* to *copious*)

---

61. **cogent** Most of the students in the audience were convinced by Dean Ohashi's <u>cogent</u> arguments.

part of speech _____ definition/synonyms _____

adj: **cogently**

---

62. **colossal** Jupiter is a <u>colossal</u> planet. More than 1,300 planets the size of Earth could fit inside of it.

part of speech _____ definition/synonyms _____

---

63. **complacent** It had been so long since the volcano had erupted that the people who lived in the village nearby grew <u>complacent</u>.

part of speech _____ definition/synonyms _____

noun: **complacence** adv: **complacently**

---

64. **complaisant** Michael and Rita's son is a pleasure to be around. He's a very <u>complaisant</u> child.

part of speech _____ definition/synonyms _____

---

65. **comply** The company was fined for not <u>complying</u> with the government's new environmental regulations.

part of speech _____ definition/synonyms _____

noun: **compliance** neg. noun: **noncompliance** adj: **compliant** neg. adj: **noncompliant**

---

66. **congenial** Magdalena Vasquez has a <u>congenial</u> personality that makes her well-suited to her job as a talk-show host.

part of speech _____ definition/synonyms _____

noun: **congeniality**

---

67. **congested** The streets of Bangkok, like those of many big cities, are <u>congested</u> with traffic.

part of speech _____ definition/synonyms _____

noun: **congestion**

---

68. **conflate** Many people <u>conflate</u> the ideas of national debt and national deficit, but they are not the same.

part of speech _____ definition/synonyms _____

---

69. **conspicuous** Since it is the only skyscraper in town, the Commonwealth Building is quite <u>conspicuous</u>.

part of speech _____ definition/synonyms _____

adv: **conspicuously**

70. **contentious** After dinner, my cousins had a loud and <u>contentious</u> discussion about the results of the election.

part of speech _____ definition/synonyms _____

verb: **contend** agent noun: **contender**

71. **contraption** In the early 1900s, airplanes were considered odd and dangerous <u>contraptions</u>.

part of speech _____ definition/synonyms _____

72. **conundrum** It is difficult to get a job without experience, and it is hard to gain experience without having a job. This is quite a <u>conundrum</u> for young job-seekers.

part of speech _____ definition/synonyms _____

73. **converge** The White Nile and the Blue Nile <u>converge</u> at the city of Khartoum in Sudan.

part of speech _____ definition/synonyms _____

noun: **convergence**

74. **convoluted** Dr. Peng's explanation was so <u>convoluted</u> and complex that it was difficult to understand.

part of speech _____ definition/synonyms _____

75. **copious** Marco took <u>copious</u> notes during Professor Owen's economics class. He filled up three entire notebooks.

part of speech _____ definition/synonyms _____

Vocabulary Exercise 5: Sentence Completion

Underline one of the two words in parentheses to create a logical sentence.

1. Two parallel lines will never (conflate/converge).

2. The road construction workers were wearing bright orange vests and bright yellow helmets so that drivers could easily see them. They wanted to be as (conspicuous/congested) as possible.

3. The lawyer gave such a (cogent/convoluted) summation of her client's contentions that the jury found in favor of her client.

4. Even though the team had won its first two games, the coach warned them not to be (complacent/complaisant). Their next game was against an even stronger opponent.

5. How do we achieve full employment without inflation? For economists, this is a major (contraption/conundrum).

6. The sidewalk near the front entrance was so (congested/conspicuous) with people trying to enter the store that we went in through the side entrance.

7. The world's largest sculpture is located in the Black Hills of South Dakota. It is a (colossal/congenial) statue of the Indian leader Crazy Horse mounted on a horse which is being carved from a mountainside.

8. He readily (conflated/complied) with the request.

9. Water-rights law in the western United States has a long, complex, and (congested/convoluted) history.

10. Sylvia said that she was tired of always acting (complacent/complaisant) and pleasant at work, and that she was finally going to stand up to her domineering boss.

Vocabulary Set 6: (*cordial* to *diatribe*)

---

76. **cordial** On the surface, those two have a <u>cordial</u> relationship, but I sense an underlying antipathy.

part of speech _____ definition/synonyms _____

noun: **cordiality** adv: **cordially**

---

77. **covert** Secret agents take part in <u>covert</u> activities.

part of speech _____ definition/synonyms _____

---

77. **craven** Some people may call him <u>craven</u>, but he just considers himself extremely cautious.

part of speech _____ definition/synonyms _____

---

78. **curb** (v.) Several new measures have been proposed to <u>curb</u> corruption among government bureaucrats.

part of speech _____ definition/synonyms _____

---

79. **cursory** Minh gave the charts in the journal only a <u>cursory</u> glance when she was in the library, but she made a copy of them so that she could examine them closely at home.

part of speech _____ definition/synonyms _____

---

80. **daunt** Although Kazuo was several strokes behind the leading golfer, he did not feel <u>daunted</u>.

part of speech _____ definition/synonyms _____

-ing adj. **daunting** neg. adjs: **undaunted**, **dauntless**

---

81. **dearth** When working on her thesis, Fatima discovered that there was a real <u>dearth</u> of information on her chosen topic, so she decided to do some research on her own.

part of speech _____ definition/synonyms _____

---

82. **deference** My grandmother always insists that, when she was a little girl, young people showed far more <u>deference</u> towards their elders.

part of speech _____ definition/synonyms _____

adj: **deferential**

---

83. **denigrate** In a formal debate, you should avoid *ad hominem* attacks. In other words, you may critique your opponents' opinions and arguments, but you should never <u>denigrate</u> them personally.

part of speech _____ definition/synonyms _____

83, **deplete** The world's supply of fossil fuels is being <u>depleted</u>.

part of speech _____ definition/synonyms _____

noun: **depletion**

84. **deplorable** Conditions in the refugee camp were <u>deplorable</u>.

part of speech _____ definition/synonyms _____

verb: **deplore** adverb: **deplorably**

85. **desiccate** Some fruit such as apricots and plums can be preserved by <u>desiccating</u> them.

part of speech _____ definition/synonyms _____

-ed adj: **desiccated**

86. **destitute** George Orwell's book *Down and Out in Paris and London* is about being <u>destitute</u> in those two cities in the 1930s.

part of speech _____ definition/synonyms _____

noun: **destitution**

87. **desultory** They had a long, rambling, <u>desultory</u> discussion, but they never really resolved any of the issues.

part of speech _____ definition/synonyms _____

88. **diatribe** The actor was supposed to give a short, pleasant acceptance speech after he won the award for his acting in a recent film, but it turned into a long, heated <u>diatribe</u> attacking the very concept of award shows such as that one.

part of speech _____ definition/synonyms _____

Vocabulary Exercise 6: Similar Sentences

If the two sentences have similar meanings, mark them **S**. If they have different meanings, mark them X.

___ 1.   A. The water in the Ogallala Aquifer has been <u>depleted</u>, especially in the last decade.
         B. There is not as much water in the aquifer as there was ten years ago.

___ 2.   A. The advertisements in this magazine are not exactly aimed at the <u>destitute</u>.
         B. The ads in the magazine target wealthier people.

___ 3.   A. The airline mechanics inspected the engines carefully.
         B. They gave the engines a <u>cursory</u> examination.

___ 4.   A. The CEO made a few <u>desultory</u> remarks to reporters after the press conference.
         B. His comments to the reporters were cogent and coherent.

___ 5.   A. The politician accused her opponent of being too <u>craven</u> to stand up to special interests
         B. According to the politician, her opponent was too fearful to take a stand against special interests.

___ 6.   A. The visitors were greeted *affably* when they arrived on the island.
         B. They were <u>cordially</u> welcomed to the island.

___ 7.   A. The meeting was so <u>covert</u> that we were not informed until the last moment when and where it would be held.
         B. Because it was a *clandestine* meeting, we were given no advance information about its location or the time at which it would be held.

___ 8.   A. The new governor announced that he would do his best to <u>curb</u> the growth of government spending.
         B. The governor intends to promote increases in government spending.

___ 9. A. There's a <u>dearth</u> of affordable rental properties close to the university
        campus.
        B. The best place for students to look for apartments to rent is near
        campus.

___ 10. A. Sergei always tries to treat his friends fairly.
        B. The way he treats his friends is <u>deplorable</u>.

Vocabulary Set 7: (*diffident* to *dissemble*)

---

91. **diffident** It's hard to believe people used to think of Ross as <u>diffident</u>—he's so full of self-confidence nowadays.
part of speech _____ definition/synonyms _____
noun: **diffidence** adv: **diffidently**

---

92. **diffuse** (v.) Politicians today use social media such as Facebook and Twitter to <u>diffuse</u> information about their campaigns.
part of speech _____ definition/synonyms _____
adj: **diffuse** noun: **diffusion**

---

93. **digress** The topic of the lecture was supposed to be sixteenth-century drama, but the speaker <u>digressed</u>. He spoke about some of his childhood experiences, about advice his parents had given him, and about several movies he had recently seen.
part of speech _____ definition/synonyms _____
noun: **digression**

---

94. **diligent** Asta is very responsible and conscientious about her studies. She is a very <u>diligent</u> student.
part of speech _____ definition/synonyms _____
noun: **diligence** adv: **diligently**

---

95. **disabuse** Janice thought she could get rich by winning the lottery. Nothing any of us could say could <u>disabuse</u> her of this notion.
part of part of speech _____ definition/synonyms _____

---

96. **discern** It is easy to <u>discern</u> the differences between an elephant and a mouse, but more difficult to differentiate between two types of elephants or two types of mice.
part of speech _____ definition/synonyms _____
-ing adj: **discerning** noun: **discernment**

---

97. **discredit** The candidate tried to <u>discredit</u> his opponent by accusing her of financial improprieties.
part of speech _____ definition/synonyms _____
noun: **discredit** -ed adj: **discredited**

98. **discreet** Michelle is not a very <u>discreet</u> person. I wouldn't tell her any secrets.
 Part of speech _____ definition/synonyms _____
The doctor didn't want anyone to know that he was a smoker, so he would only light up in <u>discreet</u> places.
noun: **discretion** neg. noun: **indiscretion** adv: **discreetly** neg. adj: **indiscreet**

99. **discrete** A basic tenet of physics and chemistry is that all matter is composed of <u>discrete</u> particles known as atoms.
part of speech _____ definition/synonyms _____

100. **disinterested** The partners cannot resolve their differences. They need a <u>dis-interested</u> party to serve as a referee.
part of speech _____ definition/synonyms _____

101. **disingenuous** I don't trust him. I think he is being <u>disingenuous</u>.
part of speech _____ definition/synonyms _____

102. **disjointed** The story was not told in chronological order, and that made it seem <u>disjointed</u>.
part of speech _____ definition/synonyms _____

103. **disparage** In her latest restaurant review, Joyce Zhou praised the food at the Blue Dolphin Restaurant, but she <u>disparaged</u> the service.
part of speech _____ definition/synonyms _____

104. **disparate** Although the two chefs had very <u>disparate</u> ideas on how to prepare food, they managed to work well together.
part of speech _____ definition/synonyms _____

105. **dissemble** The judge reminded the witness that he was still under oath, and warned him not to <u>dissemble</u>.
part of speech _____ definition/synonyms _____

Vocabulary Exercise 7: Error Check

If the sentences below are true or logical, mark them **YES**. If the sentences are false or illogical, mark them **NO**.

___ 1. The prefixes "dis-" and "un-" can both mean *not*. Therefore, "<u>disinterested</u>" and "uninterested" must have the same meaning.

___ 2. The business owner keeps her business assets and her personal assets in <u>disparate</u> accounts. This means she has a single account.

___ 3. Earl <u>dissembled</u> the lawnmower engine and then put it back together again.

___ 4. Someone who is not being completely *candid* is being <u>disingenuous</u>.

___ 5. The spies had to meet in <u>discrete</u> locations where no one could see them.

___ 6. Using linking words such as *therefore* and *nevertheless* can make your essay more <u>disjointed</u>.

___ 7. To <u>disabuse</u> someone is to treat them well.

___ 8. She was fired from her job for being such a <u>diligent</u> employee.

___ 9. To <u>diffuse</u> information is the same as to spread information.

___ 10. After a long <u>digression</u>, the lecturer finally got back on topic.

Vocabulary Set 8: (*disseminate* to *erudite*)

106. disseminate The Internet, television, radio, newspapers, magazines: These are all ways to <u>disseminate</u> information.
part of speech _____ definition/synonyms _____
noun: **dissemination**

107. divert Flights that were supposed to land in San Francisco were <u>diverted</u> to Sacramento because of thick fog at the San Francisco airport.
part of speech _____ definition/synonyms _____
noun: **diversion** -ing adj: **diverting**

108. drench He forgot to bring his raincoat or his umbrella, so by the time he got home, he was <u>drenched</u>.
part of speech _____ definition/synonyms _____

109. dwindle The couple had very little income, and their savings were <u>dwindling</u>.
part of speech _____ definition/synonyms _____

110. ebullient After learning that she'd been admitted to grad school at an Ivy League university, she was <u>ebullient</u> for the next week.
part of speech _____ definition/synonyms _____

111. eccentric My Uncle Charlie is <u>eccentric</u> in a number of ways. For example, he always brings his own silverware when he eats at a restaurant.
part of speech _____ definition/synonyms _____
noun: **eccentricity**

112. eclectic The Cosmo Café has a very <u>eclectic</u> menu with dishes from all over the world.
part of speech _____ definition/synonyms _____

113. elusive Medical scientists have searched for a cure for the common cold for years, but this goal remains <u>elusive</u>.
part of speech _____ definition/synonyms _____
verb: **elude** adv: **elusively**

114. empirical The scientific method depends on the gathering of <u>empirical</u> data.
part of speech _____ definition/synonyms _____

115. **emulate** It is common for novice artists to <u>emulate</u> the style of artists that they admire.

part of speech _____ definition/synonyms _____

noun: **emulation**

116. **enervate** After working out at the gym and taking a long, hot shower, I felt <u>enervated</u>.

part of speech _____ definition/synonyms _____

117. **engender** Severe thunderstorms sometimes <u>engender</u> tornadoes.

part of speech _____ definition/synonyms _____

118. **enigma** Deep in the Amazonian rain forest of Peru is the mysterious Boiling River, which is fed by hot springs. Hot springs warmed by underground geothermal activity are not uncommon, but those around the Boiling River are an <u>enigma</u> because they are located far from any geothermal features.

part of speech _____ definition/synonyms _____

adj. **enigmatic**

119. **ephemeral** An <u>ephemeral</u> body of water is one that exists for only a short time after a rain or snowmelt.

part of speech _____ definition/synonyms _____

120. **erudite** *A Brief History of Time* is probably the best known book by the <u>erudite</u> Stephen Hawking.

part of speech _____ definition/synonyms _____

noun: **erudition**

Vocabulary Exercise 8: Scrambled Words

Below are "scrambled" versions of ten words from Vocabulary Set 8. The letters are not in the same order as they should be. Unscramble the words by putting the letters in the correct order. Use the sentences and phrases as clues. The first one is done as an example.

1. s-l-e-i-v-u-e   Hard to find. _elusive_

2. n-g-e-i-a-m   This is mysterious—a real conundrum. _____

3. c-e-r-n-h-d   A rainstorm can do this to you. _____

4. p-l-e-r-p-m-h-a-e   Doesn't last long. _____

5. b-l-e-e-t-u-n-i-l   This is how you feel when you get good news. _____

6. e-w-i-l-d-e-n-d   Get smaller. _____

7. u-r-i-d-e-t-e   Genius. _____

9. c-e-l-t-i-c-e-c   Not the same. _____

10. l-u-t-e-t-e-m   Follow in someone's footsteps. _____

11. t-r-i-d-e-v   Reroute. _____

12. c-l-e-m-i-p-r-i-a   Based on something you see, not on something you hear about. _____

Crossword Puzzle 2: Sets 5-8 (*cogent* to *erudite*)

Across

1 Based on experiments or direct observation
3 To drain energy from; weaken; fatigue
5 Convincing; persuasive; lucid
6 Unusual; peculiar; weird
8 Hard-working; assiduous; industrious; meticulous
15 To control; limit; restrict
16 Unconnected; rambling; fragmented; confusing
17 Transitory; short-lived; temporary
18 To discourage; frighten; fill with fear

Down

1 To create; produce; make
2 To come together; merge; join; unite
3 Coming from different sources; diverse
4 Imitate; copy; follow
7 Complicated; involved; complex
9 Crowded; packed; jammed; mobbed
10 Lack; absence; scarcity; shortage
11 To shrink; decline; decrease
12 Huge; enormous; massive
13 Hard to find; difficult to catch
14 To use up; reduce; diminish
15 Cowardly; fearful; lacking courage

Vocabulary Set 9: (*esoteric* to *flamboyant*)

---

121. esoteric Ezra Pound's and T. S. Eliot's poetry contains <u>esoteric</u> references that many people today don't understand.

part of speech _____ definition/synonyms _____

---

122. exacerbate The medicine that the doctor prescribed for Jana didn't seem to make her feel any better. In fact, it may have <u>exacerbated</u> her condition.

part of speech _____ definition/synonyms _____

---

123. exculpate The evidence presented by the eye-witness served to <u>exculpate</u> the defendant, and the jury found him innocent.

part of speech _____ definition/synonyms _____

---

124. execrable The pizza they serve at Contini's Café is simply <u>execrable</u>. The crust is soggy, the sauce is tasteless, the toppings aren't fresh. Even frozen pizza tastes better.

part of speech _____ definition/synonyms _____

---

125. exigency When faced with a financial <u>exigency</u>, some people have no option other than to borrow money, sometimes at high rates of interest.

part of speech _____ definition/synonyms _____

adj: **exigent**

---

126. exotic Many Bollywood films feature scenes in <u>exotic</u> locations. Recent movies have featured scenes shot on location in Mongolia, Fiju,, and Botswana.

part of speech _____ definition/synonyms _____

---

127. facetious His comment may have sounded <u>facetious</u>, but he did raise a valid point.

part of speech _____ definition/synonyms _____

---

128. fallow For years, the land on Jim's grandparents' old farm had lain <u>fallow</u>, but this year he planted a large garden there.

part of speech _____ definition/synonyms _____

---

129. fastidious Bonnie complains that her boyfriend is not <u>fastidious</u> about his personal appearance. For example, when they went to a formal dinner party, he wore a stained tee shirt and a pair of ragged jeans.

part of speech _____ definition/synonyms _____

---

130. **fatuous** Cliff is an intelligent person, but he delights in making <u>fatuous</u> remarks.

part of speech _____ definition/synonyms _____

---

131. **feasible** The night-time lighting of large outdoor stadiums first became <u>feasible</u> in the early 1930s.

part of speech _____ definition/synonyms _____

---

132. **feckless** He claimed to be an experienced carpenter, but he proved to be quite <u>feckless</u>.

part of speech _____ definition/synonyms _____

---

133. **felicitous** The hotel I booked online turned out to be a <u>felicitous</u> choice: great location, friendly staff, and a wonderful breakfast buffet.

part of speech _____ definition/synonyms _____

---

134. **fervent** Margot is a <u>fervent</u> believer in the need for political reform.

part of speech _____ definition/synonyms _____

noun: **fervor**

---

135. **flamboyant** The Brazilian singer and actress Carmen Miranda is known for the <u>flamboyant</u> fruit-basket hats she wore in a number of movies.

part of speech _____ definition/synonyms _____

adv: **flamboyantly**

Vocabulary Exercise 9: Error Check

If the sentences below are true or logical, mark them **YES**. If the sentences are false or illogical, mark them **NO**.

____ 1. If your friend has <u>exacerbated</u> the problem, he has solved it.

____ 2. Hugh is not a <u>fastidious</u> housekeeper. In fact, his apartment is a mess.

____ 3. The artist Paul Gauguin went to Tahiti in 1890, but that was by no means his first trip to an <u>exotic</u> location.

____ 4. The farmer got a bountiful harvest from his <u>fallow</u> fields.

____ 5. He was dressed <u>flamboyantly</u> in ragged jeans, a gray sweatshirt, and a pair of old running shoes.

____ 6. <u>Feckless</u> drivers may be expert drivers, but they take far too many risks.

____ 7. <u>Esoteric</u> information is not known by many people.

____ 8. This new evidence will <u>exculpate</u> him. In other words, it will prove that he is guilty.

____ 9. A <u>facetious</u> remark is based on fact. It is truthful and clear.

____ 10. "Prepared for any <u>exigency</u>" means "ready for any emergency."

Vocabulary Set 10: (*flaunt* to *gregarious*)

136. flaunt "Name droppers" are people who like to <u>flaunt</u> the fact that they know famous people by often mentioning their names.
part of speech _____ definition/synonyms _____

137. fledgling My daughter is a <u>fledgling</u> driver. She just got her driver's license.
part of speech _____ definition/synonyms _____
agent noun: **fledgling**

138. fleeting For one <u>fleeting</u> moment, when her name was called, Vickie thought she was going to win the award, but it turned out that she came in third.
part of speech _____ definition/synonyms _____

139. flout He was sitting in the grass right in front of the "Please keep off the grass" sign, <u>flouting</u> the rule.
part of speech _____ definition/synonyms _____

140. fluke Pam has been playing chess for only a few months. She said it was just a <u>fluke</u> that she beat a much more experienced player in the student chess tournament.
part of speech _____ definition/synonyms _____

141. foolhardy Texting or playing games on your phone while driving is a <u>foolhardy</u> thing to do.
part of speech _____ definition/synonyms _____

142. forestall At the last moment, the diplomat was able to <u>forestall</u> a trade war between the two countries by getting their representatives to sign a new trade agreement.
part of speech _____ definition/synonyms _____

143. formidable One reason that the Huns were able to successfully invade the Roman Empire in the 6th century was that they possessed a <u>formidable</u> weapon that the Romans did not: a composite bow made of horn, wood, and sinew laminated together.
part of speech _____ definition/synonyms _____

144. **frivolity** Enough of this <u>frivolity</u>. Let's be serious and get down to business.
part of speech _____ definition/synonyms _____
adj: **frivolous**

145. **frugal** Mr. and Ms. McCaullie are known for being <u>frugal</u>, but they spent a fortune on their daughter's wedding.
part of speech _____ definition/synonyms _____
noun: **frugality**

146. **garrulous** I wouldn't say that Aunt Mary is <u>garrulous</u>, exactly, but she does talk quite a bit.
part of speech _____ definition/synonyms _____

147. **gaudy** Peacocks spread their <u>gaudy</u> tail feathers in order to attract a mate.
part of speech _____ definition/synonyms _____

147. **gauge** (v.) The Scoville Scale is used to <u>gauge</u> the spiciness of hot peppers.
part of speech _____ definition/synonyms _____

149. **germane** The point you brought up was interesting, but not really <u>germane</u> to today's discussion.
part of speech _____ definition/synonyms _____

150. **gregarious** Australians have a reputation for being <u>gregarious</u>, but Robert is even more sociable than most of his countrymen.
part of speech _____ definition/synonyms _____

Vocabulary Exercise 10: Fill in the Blanks

Fill in the blanks in the sentences below with one of the words from this list to form a logical sentence.

gauge	gregarious	fleeting
fluke	gaudy	foolhardy
formidable	fledgling	germane
flaunt	flout	garrulous
frivolity	frugal	frivolity

1. There are laws against shooting off fireworks on Independence Day, but many people _____ these laws.

2. The _____ taxi driver talked about politics, about the traffic, about road construction, and about his Aunt Sophie's recent surgery. He talked non-stop all the way to the airport.

3. It was difficult to _____ how much snow had fallen because it melted as soon as it fell.

4. Rosa always wears simple jewelry and dresses conservatively. She never looks _____.

5. The inspector did not give the electrical wiring a careful examination. He just gave it a _____ glance.

6. Mr. and Ms. Lopez never _____ their wealth. You'd never know they were worth more than a hundred million dollars.

7. A _____ can refer to a bird that is just learning to fly, but it can also be used to describe a person who is just learning how to do something.

8. Animals that live in groups, such as elephants or zebras, are considered _____ animals.

9. Da-Xia is not stingy or ungenerous, but she is quite _____. She hates to waste her money.

10. A ski route marked with two black diamonds is meant for the most experienced skiers, so it was quite _____ for Yoshi to ski on a double-black slope the first time he went skiing.

11. The first arrow he shot hit right in the center of the bull's-eye. However, that was apparently a _____, because the rest of his arrows missed the target entirely.

12. The "Seven Summits" is a _____ challenge. It involves climbing the highest mountains on all seven continents.

Vocabulary Set 11: (*gullible* to *impervious*)

---

151. **gullible** When it comes to deception and chicanery, there was no one better at it than the con-artist Victor Lustig. In 1925, he sold the Eiffel Tower in Paris to, not one, but two <u>gullible</u> buyers.
part of speech _____ definition/synonyms _____
noun: **gullibility**

---

152. **hamper** (v.) Work on the project was <u>hampered</u> by a lack of funds.
part of speech _____ definition/synonyms _____
neg. –ed adj: **unhampered**

---

153. **haphazard** Rather than taking a systematic approach to the problem, he took a <u>haphazard</u> approach, which, in the end, turned out to be more effective.
part of speech _____ definition/synonyms _____
adv: **haphazardly**

---

154. **harangue** A man in the park was angrily shouting at passers-by, <u>haranguing</u> anyone who would listen.
part of speech _____ definition/synonyms _____

---

155. **hasty** Don't make a <u>hasty</u> decision—think it over.
part of speech _____ definition/synonyms _____
noun: **haste** adv: **hastily**

---

156. **hazardous** It rained all afternoon, and then night-time temperatures dropped well below freezing. The roads were coated with a sheet of ice, creating <u>hazardous</u> driving conditions.
part of speech _____ definition/synonyms _____

---

157. **hegemony** It was during the reign of the Emperor Patchacuti, which began in 1440, that the Incans established <u>hegemony</u> over much of South America west of the Andes Mountains.
part of speech _____ definition/synonyms _____

---

158. **hiatus** After a four-month <u>hiatus</u>, the play will re-open at an off-Broadway theater.
part of speech _____ definition/synonyms _____

---

159. **hinder** Johan was running to catch the bus, but he was <u>hindered</u> by the heavy package he was carrying.
part of speech _____ definition/synonyms _____
noun: **hindrance** neg. –ed adj: **unhindered**

160. **hoax** In 1835, a series of articles appeared in the *New York Sun* describing what the respected astronomer Sir John Hershel had seen when examining the Moon with a powerful new telescope. The articles said Hershel had seen unicorns, intelligent beavers that walked on two legs, and people with wings like bats. Hershel declared that the stories were a <u>hoax</u>, but newspapers worldwide reprinted them, and they were widely believed.
part of speech _____ definition/synonyms _____

161. **humdrum** James Thurber's story "The Secret Life of Walter Mitty" is about a man who escapes his <u>humdrum</u> existence by dreaming up wild and adventurous fantasies starring himself.
part of speech _____ definition/synonyms _____

162. **impassive** Her expression was <u>impassive</u>, but I know she must have found the news disturbing.
part of speech _____ definition/synonyms _____
adv: **impassively**

163. **impecunious** I am afraid I find myself <u>impecunious</u>, at least until I get my pay check on Friday.
part of speech _____ definition/synonyms _____

164. **imperious** The ship's captain shouted out his orders in an <u>imperious</u> tone of voice.
part of speech _____ definition/synonyms _____
adv: **imperiously**

165. **impervious** Some ceramics are completely <u>impervious</u> to acids, even to hot, highly concentrated sulfuric acid.
part of speech _____ definition/synonyms _____

Vocabulary Exercise 11: Similar Sentences

If the two sentences have similar meanings, mark them **S**. If they have different meanings, mark them **X**.

____ 1.   A. The storm <u>hampered</u> the efforts of the search party.
          B. The storm <u>hindered</u> the search, making it more difficult.

____ 2.   A. I received an email saying that I was going to inherit a lot of money from a relative I'd never heard of, but unfortunately, it turned out to be a <u>hoax</u>.
          B. Sadly, I didn't receive any money.

____ 3.   A. He listened <u>impassively</u> to what his father told him.
          B. He was clearly excited by what his father said.

____ 4.   A. The family <u>hastily</u> prepared to leave the city.
          B. They had been planning the trip for a long time.

____ 5.   A. Shooting at Superman doesn't hurt him a bit.
          B. Superman is <u>impervious</u> to bullets.

____ 6.   A. David said he was going to take us all out to dinner at an expensive restaurant because he recently came into some money.
          B. David is going to take us to dinner because he's feeling <u>impecunious</u>.

____ 7.   A. I really thought this was going to be another <u>humdrum</u> evening.
          B. I expected that we were going to have some excitement this evening.

____ 8.   A. Paul takes a <u>haphazard</u> approach to cooking.
          B. The way Paul prepares food could actually be dangerous.

____ 9.   A. There are some people who believe anything they read on the Internet.
          B. There are some very <u>gullible</u> people in this world.

____ 10. A. Every night, the radio talk-show host <u>harangues</u> his listeners.
          B. The talk-show host's commentaries are always calm, cogent, and thoughtful.

Vocabulary Set 12: (*importune* to *intrepid*)

166. importune   The alumni association of the university I attended often importunes me to donate money to the university.
part of speech _____ definition/synonyms _____
adj: **importunate**

167. impromptu With no time to prepare any remarks, the chancellor had to give an impromptu speech.
part of speech _____ definition/synonyms _____

168. impulsive Marcella made an impulsive decision to buy a car without doing any research or speaking to her mechanic.
part of speech _____ definition/synonyms _____
noun: **impulse** adv: **impulsively**

169. inadvertent I had no intention of going into the swimming pool. It was completely inadvertent.
part of speech _____ definition/synonyms _____
adv: **inadvertently**

170. inchoate   In the mid-twentieth century, computer science was still in its inchoate stage.
 part of speech _____ definition/synonyms _____

171. incisive He has a clear, incisive style of writing, but he is not a particularly eloquent speaker.
part of speech _____ definition/synonyms _____
adv: **incisively**

172. indigent Abraham Lincoln's family was almost indigent when he was a child, and he lived his first few years in a tiny, one-room log cabin.
part of speech _____ definition/synonyms _____
noun: **indigence**

173. incongruous The modern addition to the old Victorian home seemed quite incongruous.
part of speech _____ definition/synonyms _____
noun: **incongruity** adv: **incongruously**

174. **indifferent** Elsa is completely <u>indifferent</u> when it comes to campus politics. She doesn't care at all who is elected president of the student council.
part of speech _____ definition/synonyms _____
noun: **indifference** adv: **indifferently**

175. **inept** I've always been <u>inept</u> at guessing people's ages, so when Martha asked me how old I thought she was, I declined to guess.
part of speech _____ definition/synonyms _____

176. **infamous** A number of the Roman emperors are <u>infamous</u> for their cruelty, but Marcus Aurelius was well-known for being a benevolent ruler and a prominent philosopher.
part of speech _____ definition/synonyms _____

177. **ingenious** Harie, Japan's "village of living water," has come up with an <u>ingenious</u> way of providing its people and their crops with fresh, clean water.
part of speech _____ definition/synonyms _____

178. **insinuate** Luiza hates when people <u>insinuate</u> things about her. She wishes they would just come out and say what they really think of her.
part of speech _____ definition/synonyms _____
noun: **insinuation**

179. **insipid** What a boring, ridiculous movie. I hate when I waste money on <u>insipid</u> films.
part of speech _____ definition/synonyms _____

180. **insular** He grew up in a small village in the mountains where most people had an <u>insular</u> attitude.
part of speech _____ definition/synonyms _____

Vocabulary Exercise 12: Matching

Match these words with their synonyms.

1. inadvertent ___

2. insinuate ___

3. impulsive ___

4. inchoate ___

5. insipid ___

6. incongruous ___

7. impromptu ___

8. inept ___

9. importune ___

10. incisive ___

11. indigent ___

12. infamous ___

A. Inconsistent; unsuitable; inappropriate; not blending in

B. Unintentional; accidental; involuntary

C. Incompetent; feckless; lacking skill or ability; clumsy

D. Notorious; disreputable; well known for negative reasons

E. To request; beg; solicit; implore; pester; harass

F. To imply something negative

G. Bland; uninteresting; unexciting; banal; lacking flavor

H. Perceptive; sharp; insightful; trenchant

I. Poor; penurious; impoverished

J. Unplanned; unrehearsed; off the cuff

K. Capricious; spontaneous; whimsical; impetuous

L. Undeveloped; unfinished; incipient; not fully formed

Crossword Puzzle 3: Sets 9-12 (*esoteric* to *intrepid*)

Across

1 To show off; exhibit so that other people will notice; display in an ostentatious way
3 Showy; flamboyant; colorful
4 Capricious; whimsical; acting without a plan
5 To measure; appraise
6 Commanding; domineering; authoritarian
7 Talkative; verbose; loquacious
9 A stroke of luck; a chance occurrence; a coincidence
11 Unusual but interesting; fascinating
13 Thrifty; careful with money
15 Unintentional; involuntary; accidental
16 Lacking ability or talent; incompetent; feckless

Down

1 Quick; momentary; transitory
2 Uncultivated; unplanted
3 Sociable; friendly; outgoing
4 Poor; penniless; indigent; broke
8 Gaudy; showy; flashy; colorful
9 Levity; humor; comedy; light-heartedness
10 To free from guilt; prove innocent; exonerate
11 Obscure; recondite; known to only a few people
12 To hinder; obstruct; restrict; impede
14 Trick; fraud; deception

Vocabulary Set 13: (*irascible* to *lethargic*)

---

181. **intrepid**   Far and Away Adventure Tours is not for tourists whose idea of a vacation is to sit on a beach. It is for <u>intrepid</u> travelers who want to explore exotic locations and face challenges.

part of speech _____   definition/synonyms _____

---

182. **invaluable**   My academic advisor gave me some <u>invaluable</u> advice that helped me get into the grad school that I was most interested in.

part of speech _____   definition/synonyms _____

---

183. **invigorate**   Some people find a cold shower <u>invigorating</u>, while others prefer a warm bath.

part of speech _____   definition/synonyms _____

-ing adj: **invigorating** noun: **vigor**

---

184. **irascible**   My grandfather is pretty <u>irascible</u> in the morning, at least until he has had his first cup of coffee.

part of speech _____   definition/synonyms _____

---

185. **itinerant**   <u>Itinerant</u> groups of people have often been a source of suspicion to sedentary people.

part of speech _____   definition/synonyms _____

---

186. **jargon**   Whenever I have a problem with my computer, I ask my friend Tomas for help, but he uses so much computer <u>jargon</u> that I find it hard to follow his explanation. It's as if he's speaking another language.

part of speech _____   definition/synonyms _____

---

187. **juxtapose**   If you <u>juxtapose</u> a map of Indonesia across a map of the United States, you will see that the distance from one end of the archipelago to the other is farther than the distance from New York to San Francisco.

part of speech _____   definition/synonyms _____

noun: **juxtaposition**

---

188. **knack**   Anyone can cook simple dishes. You don't need a special <u>knack</u>.

part of speech _____   definition/synonyms _____

---

189. **lackadaisical** Erica likes people to think that she is <u>lackadaisical</u> about her studies, but she is actually a very serious student.

part of speech _____ definition/synonyms _____

190. **laconic** We expected him to make a long after-dinner speech, but tonight, he was uncharacteristically <u>laconic</u>.

part of speech _____ definition/synonyms _____

191. **lamentable** The speaker said that students' lack of knowledge about history was quite <u>lamentable</u>.

part of speech _____ definition/synonyms _____
verb: **lament** adv: **lamentably**

192. **languish** Although the study of astronomy <u>languished</u> in Europe during the Middle Ages, it flourished among the Arabs.

part of speech _____ definition/synonyms _____

193. **lassitude** Symptoms of hypothermia—the extreme loss of body heat—include confusion, apathy, and <u>lassitude</u>, creating an almost irresistible desire to lie down and go to sleep.

part of speech _____ definition/synonyms _____

194. **lax** There are some tough regulations against smoking anywhere on campus, but enforcement of these rules is <u>lax</u>.

part of speech _____ definition/synonyms _____
noun: **laxity**

195. **lethargic** I'm feeling pretty <u>lethargic</u> this afternoon. I either need to get a cup of coffee or take a nap.

part of speech _____ definition/synonyms _____
noun: **lethargy**

Vocabulary Exercise 13: Multiple Choice

Choose the word or words that are closest in meaning to the underlined word.

1. Phil was in an <u>irascible</u> mood after he got that phone call from his girlfriend.
   A. light-hearted   B. grumpy   C. relaxed

2. His failure taught him <u>an invaluable</u> lesson.
   A. a worthless   B. a significant   C. an irrelevant

3. Work on this project <u>languished</u> until Ms. Pham became the project manager.
   A. did not progress   B. was not begun   C. went forward quickly

4. Professor Lyons said that recent changes in university policy adopted by the administration were quite <u>lamentable</u>.
   A. unexpected   B. encouraging   C. regrettable

5. Svetlana has a <u>knack</u> for doing academic research.
   A. talent   B. distaste   C. system

6. Every occupation and academic field has its own <u>jargon</u>.
   A. mythology   B. terminology   C. methodology

7. His <u>laconic</u> response surprised everyone.
   A. brief   B. emotional   C. detailed

8. After a long game of beach volleyball, we all felt <u>lethargic</u>.
   A. energized   B. overheated   C. enervated

9. Mr. Braun feels that many of the problems that exist today are caused by the fact that parents are too <u>lax</u>.
   A. too busy   B. not strict enough   C. too controlling

10. My Uncle Louis was an <u>itinerant</u> salesman.
    A. successful   B. clever   C. traveling

Vocabulary Set 14: (*levity* to *meticulous*)

196. **levity** The mood of <u>levity</u> at the staff meeting soon gave way to one of anxiety as the managing director announced that there would be lay-offs next month.
part of speech _____ definition/synonyms _____

197. **lionize** Muhammad Ali was <u>lionized</u>, not just by boxing fans but by people all over the world.
part of speech _____ definition/synonyms _____

198. **loquacious** Nineteenth-century politicians generally tended to be much more <u>loquacious</u> than present-day politicians. Their speeches often went on for hours and hours.
part of speech _____ definition/synonyms _____

199. **lucid** Although she had barely survived a disaster, she was able to give a remarkably <u>lucid</u> account of what had happened.
part of speech _____ definition/synonyms _____
noun: **lucidity** adv: **lucidly**

200. **lucrative** Fishing in the Atlantic in Colonial times was a <u>lucrative</u> profession, but then as now, it was extremely dangerous.
part of speech _____ definition/synonyms _____

201. **ludicrous** She said she thought it was <u>ludicrous</u> that sports stars and entertainers were paid so much more than teachers and nurses.
part of speech _____ definition/synonyms _____

202. **lugubrious** Portuguese Fado songs often have <u>lugubrious</u> lyrics about the plight of poor people or about the loss of love.
part of speech _____ definition/synonyms _____

203. **luminous** The Moon is <u>luminous</u> only because it reflects the light of the Sun.
part of speech _____ definition/synonyms _____
noun: **luminosity**

204. **malodorous** There was a <u>malodorous</u> scent coming from the chemistry lab. It smelled almost like rotten eggs.
part of speech _____ definition/synonyms _____

205. **mar** Someone had used a sharp instrument—perhaps a screwdriver or a knife—to <u>mar</u> the surface of the antique desk.
part of speech _____ definition/synonyms _____

206. **meander** The path <u>meanders</u> through the park, turning this way and that, and then doubling back on itself.
part of speech _____ definition/synonyms _____
-ing adj: **meandering**

207. **mediocre** Caroline said she was only a <u>mediocre</u> singer, but I think she has a beautiful voice.
part of speech _____ definition/synonyms _____
noun: **mediocrity**

208. **mendacious** Lie detector tests, when administered by a skilled operator, can often determine if a person is being <u>mendacious</u>.
part of speech _____ definition/synonyms _____

209. **mercurial** The opera singer was well known for his <u>mercurial</u> personality. His mood changed at least hourly.
part of speech _____ definition/synonyms _____

210. **meticulous** Pareesh's instructor asked him to rewrite the bibliography for his research paper. This time, he did a <u>meticulous</u> job, following the guidelines in the style manual exactly.
part of speech _____ definition/synonyms _____
adv: **meticulously**

Vocabulary Exercise 14: Fill in the Blanks

Fill in the blanks in the sentences below with one of the words from this list to form a logical sentence.

meticulous	lucid	lucrative
meandered	marred	lugubrious
mediocre	lionize	mendacious
luminosity	loquacious	malodorous

1. My family and I took a month-long road trip in the United States one summer when I was a kid. We _____ through all the western states, wandering from one national park to another, and stopping anywhere that we thought sounded interesting.

2. Even when Wally is happy, his perpetually sad expression and the way he shuffles along give him a _____ air.

3. The trash collectors had been on strike for two weeks, and on every downtown sidewalk, huge piles of bags full of _____ garbage sat out in the hot sun.

4. He told a clumsy lie to explain why he shouldn't be blamed for his role in the problem, but everyone knew he was being _____.

5. The team almost had a perfect season, but their record was _____ by the fact that they lost their final match.

6. Ms. Chaiprasit is an excellent technical writer. The instructional manuals she writes for electronic devices are _____ and easy to follow.

7. Sally was promoted and given a raise because she did a _____ job training the new employees.

8. What astronomers call the brightness of a star is a measure of how bright it appears from Earth. However, the _____ of a star is a true, intrinsic measurement of how much light the star actually produces.

9. I was told the Riverside Bistro was a _____ restaurant, but I had a wonderful dinner there last night.

10. The author's young fans _____ her. They think her books are even more entertaining than the Harry Potter series.

Vocabulary Set 15: (*minute* to *nostalgic*)

---

211. **minute** (adj) Our bodies need large amounts of macronutrients—carbohydrates, proteins, fats, and water. However, we need only <u>minute</u> amounts of micronutrients such as vitamins and minerals.
part of speech _____ definition/synonyms _____

---

212. **miserly** I never realized how <u>miserly</u> Mr. Schmidt was until he refused to leave a tip for the waiter.
part of speech _____ definition/synonyms _____
agent noun: **miser**

---

213. **mitigate** The company has taken several steps to <u>mitigate</u> the negative effects of emissions from its factories, but so far, these efforts have not been very successful.
part of speech _____ definition/synonyms _____
-ing adj: **mitigating**

---

214. **mollify** Annika was furious, and nothing anyone could say or do would <u>mollify</u> her.
part of speech _____ definition/synonyms _____

---

215. **mordant** The architect's plans for a huge new office complex faced some <u>mordant</u> criticism in the local newspaper.
part of speech _____ definition/synonyms _____

---

216. **moribund** Today, the shopping mall is <u>moribund</u>. It was bustling and busy ten years ago, but now there are only a handful of shops still open.
part of speech _____ definition/synonyms _____

---

217. **morose** Within the last week, Stephano lost his job, his girlfriend left him, and his dog ran away. No wonder he is <u>morose</u>.
part of speech _____ definition/synonyms _____
adv: **morosely**

---

218. **mundane** When I'm doing <u>mundane</u> tasks like washing the dishes or vacuuming the carpets, I put on my earphones and listen to music. It makes these tasks seem much more bearable.
part of speech _____ definition/synonyms _____

219. **mushroom** (v.) Because of the discovery of huge natural gas deposits nearby, Seaton City has become a boomtown and its population is <u>mushrooming</u>.
part of speech _____ definition/synonyms _____

220. **myriad** Sailors on fishing boats do not have one single job to do. They have <u>myriad</u> tasks.
part of speech _____ definition/synonyms _____

221. **mythical** For many years, people believed that giant squids were entirely <u>mythical</u>. It wasn't until Japanese researchers photographed a giant squid in 2006 that there was definite proof that these deep-sea creatures actually existed.
part of speech _____ definition/synonyms _____
nouns: **mythology, myth**

222. **neophyte** This cake looks like it was baked by a real <u>neophyte</u>, not by a professional baker.
part of speech _____ definition/synonyms _____

223. **noisome** Because of the broken sewage line, the entire neighborhood was filled with a <u>noisome</u> smell.
part of speech _____ definition/synonyms _____

224. **nonchalant** I knew Mariko was nervous, but as she approached the podium to deliver the graduation speech, she seemed to be completely <u>nonchalant</u>.
part of speech _____ definition/synonyms _____
noun: **nonchalance** adv: **nonchalantly**

225. **nostalgic** Listening to these songs from the 1990s makes me <u>nostalgic</u>.
part of speech _____ definition/synonyms _____
noun: **nostalgia**

Vocabulary Exercise 15: Similar Sentences

If the two sentences have similar meanings, mark them **S**. If they have different meanings, mark them **X**.

___ 1.   A. If they ask you any questions, try to be <u>nonchalant</u>.
           B. Don't be nervous if they question you.

___ 2.   A. That music was far too loud! It hurt my ears.
           B. It was absolutely <u>noisome</u>.

___ 3.   A. Danny was <u>morose</u>.
           B. He was sad and upset.

___ 4.   A. Although he was relatively inexperienced, he was not a <u>neophyte</u>.
           B. He was still considered a fledgling.

___ 5.   A. This problem is starting to <u>mushroom</u>.
           B. The problem is becoming more and more severe.

___ 6.   A. Since she was a philosophy major, Marika seldom spoke of <u>mundane</u> matters.
           B. Marika didn't talk about ordinary affairs because she was majoring in philosophy.

___ 7.   A. Unicorns, centaurs, and griffins are purely <u>mythical</u> beasts.
           B. These animals are rarely seen these days.

___ 8.   A. Many languages around the world today are used only by a few elderly speakers.
           B. Worldwide, many languages have become <u>moribund</u>.

___ 9.   A. Valeria was quite <u>nostalgic</u> for her home country.
           B. She was feeling very homesick.

___ 10.   A. A <u>minute</u> amount of dust can damage a computer's hard drive.
           B. Even a few grains of dust can destroy the hard drive on a computer.

Vocabulary Set 16: (*notorious* to *palpable*)

226. **notorious** New York City was once <u>notorious</u> for its high crime rate, but that rate has been dropping since the mid-1990s and, since 2015, it has been lower than the national average.

part of speech _____ definition/synonyms _____

noun: **notoriety**

---

227. **obdurate** Ms. Oh was being <u>obdurate</u>. She wouldn't compromise or give in on any point.

part of speech _____ definition/synonyms _____

---

228. **oblivious** We were <u>oblivious</u> to the passing of time. We had no idea that it was almost dawn.

part of speech _____ definition/synonyms _____

---

229. **obtuse** When we failed to agree with him, Antoine accused us of being <u>obtuse</u>.

part of speech _____ definition/synonyms _____

---

230. **obviate** The university gave Johan a full scholarship to study astrophysics. This <u>obviated</u> the need for him to take out a student loan from the bank.

part of speech _____ definition/synonyms _____

---

231. **officious** The <u>officious</u> customs agent asked us question after question and then demanded that we open our suitcases.

part of speech _____ definition/synonyms _____

noun: **officiousness**

---

232. **onerous** Although there are many tools to make farmers' work easier that it was in the past, farming is still an <u>onerous</u> job.

part of speech _____ definition/synonyms _____

---

233. **orthodox** Many young entrepreneurs are disregarding the <u>orthodox</u> theories about how to run a business.

part of speech _____ definition/synonyms _____

noun: **orthodoxy** negative adj: **unorthodox**

234. **ostentatious** The billionaire had an enormous, <u>ostentatious</u> yacht anchored in front of the hotel that he owned.

part of speech _____ definition/synonyms _____

noun: **ostentation**

---

233. **oversee** Endang <u>oversees</u> a staff of ten office workers.

part of speech _____ definition/synonyms _____

agent noun: **overseer**

---

236. **overt** She made no effort to conceal her disappointment. She was completely <u>overt</u> about it.

part of speech _____ definition/synonyms _____

adv: **overtly**

---

237. **pacify** The students and their parents were outraged about the huge increase in tuition costs. The letter that the president of the university wrote explaining the need for the increase did nothing to <u>pacify</u> them.

part of speech _____ definition/synonyms _____

noun: **pacification**

---

238. **paucity** The admissions department said there was no <u>paucity</u> of applications from qualified candidates this year.

part of speech _____ definition/synonyms _____

---

239. **pedestrian** (adj) The set-designer's work in the past had been rather <u>pedestrian</u>, but the sets he designed for Shakespeare in the Park were imaginative and breathtaking.

part of speech _____ definition/synonyms _____

---

240. **palpable** There was a <u>palpable</u> sense of anxiety in the room.

part of speech _____ definition/synonyms _____

Vocabulary Exercise 16: Matching

Match these words with their synonyms.

1. palpable ___	A. infamous; famous for being wicked
2. ostentatious ___	B. banal; boring; commonplace
3. orthodox ___	C. to preclude; prevent; eliminate the need for
4. pedestrian ___	D. showy; flamboyant; flashy; gaudy
5. onerous ___	E. arduous; difficult; challenging
6. obtuse ___	F. dense; simple-minded; unperceptive
7. paucity ___	G. lack; absence; dearth
8. obviate ___	H. obvious; clear; open; explicit
9. oversee ___	I. to direct; supervise; manage
10. notorious ___	J. tangible; real; perceptible; able to be felt
11. pacify ___	K. traditional; standard; accepted; conventional
12. overt ___	L. to calm; soothe; appease; mollify; placate

Crossword Puzzle 4: Sets 13-16 (*irascible* to *palpable*)

Across

1 Quiet; silent; not talkative
3 Bright; shining; emitting light
6 Clear; understandable; articulate
7 Depressed; upset; sad
11 Priceless; precious; vital
15 Stubborn; obstinate; uncompromising; inflexible; pertinacious
16 Damage; deface; ruin
17 To energize; strengthen; empower
18 To manage; supervise; direct

Down

1 Not enforcing rules; careless; not strict
2 Traveling; wandering; nomadic; peripatetic
3 Light-heartedness; frivolity; comedy
4 Tiny; miniscule; very small
5 Beginner; fledgling; novice; tyro
7 To expand quickly; burgeon; grow rapidly
8 Special talent or ability; aptitude
9 Ridiculous; absurd
10 Foul-smelling; rank; stinky
12 Profitable; rewarding; producing income
13 Banal; ordinary; boring; quotidian
14 Declining; dying; on its way out

Vocabulary Set 17: (*parched* to *plush*)

---

241. **parched** After three years of drought, the land was <u>parched</u>.
part of speech _____ definition/synonyms _____

---

242. **pensive** Jean-Charles was in a <u>pensive</u> mood this afternoon, so he went off to sit by the river and think deep thoughts.
part of speech _____ definition/synonyms _____

---

243. **penurious** He arrived in this country a <u>penurious</u> young man. Forty years later, he still has no money.
part of speech _____ definition/synonyms _____

---

244. **perfunctory** The pianist gave the sheet music a <u>perfunctory</u> glance and said of course he could play that song.
part of speech _____ definition/synonyms _____

---

245. **perilous** In his book *Lewis and Clark Among the Grizzly Bears*, author Paul Schullery recounts the explorers' <u>perilous</u> encounters with these huge, magnificent, and dangerous creatures.
part of speech _____ definition/synonyms _____
noun: **peril** verb: **imperil** adv: **perilously**

---

246. **peripheral** A <u>peripheral</u> device, such as a mouse, keyboard, printer, or scanner, is connected to a computer system but does not contribute directly to the computer's primary functions.
part of speech _____ definition/synonyms _____
noun: **periphery** adv: **peripherally**

---

247. **petulant** Lucy and Tim's daughter becomes sullen and <u>petulant</u> and stamps her feet whenever she doesn't get her way.
part of speech _____ definition/synonyms _____
noun: **petulance** adv: **petulantly**

---

248. **pithy** My father gave me some <u>pithy</u> advice when I went away to college: "Don't take any classes before nine o'clock or above the second floor."
part of speech _____ definition/synonyms _____

---

249. **pivotal** A trumpet player, composer, and singer, Louis Armstrong played a pivotal role in the development of jazz.
part of speech _____ definition/synonyms _____

250. **placate** Although Ian had reserved a room weeks before, there was none available when he arrived at the hotel. The clerk apologized and offered to help him find a room in another hotel, but her offer did nothing to placate Ian.
part of speech _____ definition/synonyms _____

251. **plethora** He already had a plethora of problems; now he has one more.
part of speech _____ definition/synonyms _____

252. **plight** In *Oliver Twist*, Charles Dickens wrote about the plight of homeless orphans in Victorian London.
part of speech _____ definition/synonyms _____

253. **plummet** Mr. Prideaux predicted that the cost of a barrel of oil would plummet, but in fact, it only went down by a few cents a barrel.
part of speech _____ definition/synonyms _____

254. **plunge** The La Quebrada Cliff Divers are a group of professional divers based in Acapulco, Mexico. They perform daily shows for the public, which involve diving from high cliffs and plunging into the Pacific Ocean far below.
part of speech _____ definition/synonyms _____
noun: **plunge** adjective: **plunging**

255. **plush** By the 1830s, there were around 1200 steamboats on the Mississippi River. The furnishings on some of them were as plush as those found in the most luxurious hotels of the time.
part of speech _____ definition/synonyms _____

Vocabulary Exercise 17: Similar Sentences

If the two sentences have similar meanings, mark them **S**. If they have different meanings, mark them **X**.

1. ___　A. In the fall of 2008, housing prices <u>plummeted</u>.
　　　　　B. The costs of houses <u>plunged</u> in the autumn of 2008.

2. ___　A. As graduation approached, Leo grew more <u>pensive</u> than usual.
　　　　　B. Since he was about to graduate, Leo became more and more excited.

3. ___　A. An aphorism is a <u>pithy</u> piece of advice.
　　　　　B. Aphorisms are long, detailed articles that provide guidance.

4. ___　A. In the past, the dining cars on passenger trains were quite luxurious.
　　　　　B. Passenger trains once offered meals in <u>plush</u> surroundings.

5. ___　A. Ms. Singh played a <u>pivotal</u> role in the development of this app.
　　　　　B. Ms. Singh's role in the development of this app was a <u>peripheral</u> one.

6. ___　A. This article offers a <u>plethora</u> of ideas for home entertainment.
　　　　　B. There are plenty of ideas about entertaining at home in this article.

7. ___　A. I just finished watering the plants in my garden.
　　　　　B. The soil in my garden is <u>parched</u> now.

8. ___　A. This video clearly shows the terrible <u>plight</u> of the refugees.
　　　　　B. The desperate conditions that the refugees face are clearly shown in this video.

9. ___　A. An offer to go to dinner at a wonderful restaurant might help to <u>placate</u> him.
　　　　　B. A chance to go do dinner at a superb restaurant may make him feel better.

10. ___　A. Andrew is a <u>petulant</u> young man.
　　　　　B. Andrew is always smiling and laughing.

Vocabulary Set 18: (*precarious* to *quaint*)

256. **precarious** I wouldn't want a job washing the windows of a skyscraper. Those platforms where the window-washers work look so <u>precarious</u> to me.
part of speech _____ definition/synonyms _____

257. **preclude** The fact that the defendant is Judge Ogawa's niece <u>precludes</u> him from hearing the case.
part of speech _____ definition/synonyms _____

258. **preposterous** I read in this magazine that some celebrities pay more than a thousand dollars for a haircut. That seems utterly <u>preposterous</u> to me.
part of speech _____ definition/synonyms _____

259. **prescient** Psychics claim to be <u>prescient</u>. They say they know what will happen before it actually happens.
part of speech _____ definition/synonyms _____

260. **prevaricate** Mitch said he was at home and was sound asleep at the time of the incident, but the detective suspected that he was <u>prevaricating</u>.
part of speech _____ definition/synonyms _____
noun: **prevarication**

261. **pristine** Today, Isla Nubar is a <u>pristine</u> tropical island with white sand beaches, turquoise waters, and lots of seabirds. However, there are plans to develop it into a resort with an airport, a cruise-ship dock, several hotels. and an amusement park.
part of speech _____ definition/synonyms _____

262. **prodigious** The huge Saturn rockets that carried astronauts to the Moon burned <u>prodigious</u> amounts of liquid fuel during the take-off stage.
part of speech _____ definition/synonyms _____

263. **profligate** When their credit card statement arrived, the couple regretted their <u>profligate</u> spending on their vacation.
part of speech _____ definition/synonyms _____

264. **prolific** Agatha Christie was a <u>prolific</u> writer. Between 1920 and 1970, she wrote 70 novels and 19 plays, and she sold more than five billion books
part of speech _____ definition/synonyms _____

265. **prolix** When the journalist moved from a print magazine to an on-line magazine, he was told by the editor to write shorter pieces. She told him that a ten-page article might be fine in a print magazine, but it was just too prolix for most readers on an Internet site.
part of speech _____ definition/synonyms _____

266. **propitious** Flights to Paris are cheaper than they have been in years. This might be a propitious time for a European vacation.
part of speech _____ definition/synonyms _____

267. **prosaic** Normally a novelist, Monique Breaux has begun writing a series of travel guides. The first covers Southeast Asia. There is some lively language and some brilliant insights, but there also some long, prosaic descriptions of hotels, restaurants, and airports.
part of speech _____ definition/synonyms _____

268. **puerile** I know Stewart is a brilliant scientist, but in social situations, he sometimes seems unsophisticated and puerile.
part of speech _____ definition/synonyms _____

269. **pungent** Years ago, I had an apartment in a building behind a seafood restaurant. On hot summer days, the pungent smell of spoiled fish would permeate our building.
part of speech _____ definition/synonyms _____

270. **quaint** Ned owns a quaint little bookstore on Beacon Hill in Boston. When you walk in, you feel like you are in another century.
part of speech _____ definition/synonyms _____

Vocabulary Exercise 18: Fill in the Blanks

Fill in the blanks in the sentences below with one of the words from this list to form a logical sentence.

puerile	prolix	preposterous
pungent	propitious	prescient
perilous	preclude	prolific
prodigious	prosaic	prevaricate

1. Picasso was an exceptionally _____ artist. His lifetime output includes more than 20,000 paintings, prints, and drawings.

2. The fact that you are majoring in economics does not _____ you from taking a few liberal arts courses such as literature or art history.

3. Harold has a _____ sense of humor. He's always telling immature jokes and playing pranks.

4. I had an important meeting on Friday. When I woke up, the sun was shining, birds were singing, and I smelled coffee being brewed. I took these as _____ signs that things would go well for me.

5. The chief financial officer warned the board of directors that the firm was in a _____ financial situation and that it might be necessary to lay off some employees.

6. In the fifteenth century, the idea that people could fly like birds must have seemed _____. That didn't stop Leonardo Da Vinci from dreaming of manned flight and designing flying machines.

7. Many people get too caught up in _____, day-to-day concerns to worry much about the future of the planet.

8. The speaker could easily have cut the length of his speech from an hour to a half hour. He was far too _____.

9. Sulfur is what gives onions their _____ taste. Because the soil in south Georgia has little sulfur, Vidalia onions are sweeter and less spicy than most onions.

10. Twenty years ago, the historian Howard Zinn was asked to make some predictions about the future, many of which turned out to be quite_____.

Vocabulary Set 19: (*qualm* to *restive*)

---

271. **qualm** Peter had some <u>qualms</u> about leaving the band, but he believed he would be far more successful as a solo musician.
part of speech _____ definition/synonyms _____

---

272. **quandary** Esma was accepted at two top grad schools, one in the US and one in Canada. This presented her with a real <u>quandary</u>.
part of speech _____ definition/synonyms _____

---

273. **querulous** As everyone knows, he is quite a <u>querulous</u> individual. Paradoxically, he often begins his sentences by saying, "I hate to complain, but ..."
part of speech _____ definition/synonyms _____

---

274. **quibble** I don't want to <u>quibble</u> about this, so let's just do it your way.
part of speech _____ definition/synonyms _____
noun: **quibble**

---

275 **quiescent** The period from 1817 to 1835 was a relatively <u>quiescent</u> and prosperous time in U.S. history. In fact, it is sometimes called "the era of good feelings."
part of speech _____ definition/synonyms _____
noun: **quiescence**

---

276. **quirk** My friend Alex has a few odd <u>quirks</u>. For example, when he is at a supermarket or a big-box store, and he notices that an item has been misplaced, he feels compelled to return that item to its proper shelf.
part of speech _____ definition/synonyms _____
adj: **quirky**

---

277. **quotidian** Tired of his <u>quotidian</u> existence, Wim sold everything he owned and set off on a round-the-world journey.
part of speech _____ definition/synonyms _____

---

278. **rapacious** Mr. Dimitrou was forced to relocate his café because his <u>rapacious</u> landlord kept raising his rent.
part of speech _____ definition/synonyms _____

---

279. **rash** I know you are upset, but don't do anything <u>rash</u>. Calm down and think things over.
part of speech _____ definition/synonyms _____
adv: **rashly**

---

280. **raucous** Crows are large black birds with a <u>raucous</u> cry. In fact, the word *crow* comes from the Old English word *crawe*, which imitates the sound that the bird makes.

part of speech _____ definition/synonyms _____

281. **rebound** After decades of losing people to the suburbs, the population of many large cities has begun to <u>rebound</u>.

part of speech _____ definition/synonyms _____

282. **recalcitrant** The prisoner remained <u>recalcitrant</u>, refusing to answer questions or to cooperate in any way.

part of speech _____ definition/synonyms _____

noun: **recalcitrance**

283. **recondite** I tried to read that article about black holes that Professor Kuo recommended, but it found most of the information in the article quite <u>recondite</u>.

part of speech _____ definition/synonyms _____

284. **relish** (v.) I don't <u>relish</u> another winter storm. I'm tired of all this snow and cold weather.

part of speech _____ definition/synonyms _____

285. **restive** Although there was no open revolt, the people in the northern provinces remained <u>restive</u>.

part of speech _____ definition/synonyms _____

Vocabulary Exercise 19: Error Check

If the sentences below are true or logical, mark them **YES**. If the sentences are false or illogical, mark them **NO**.

___ 1. Cheryl is <u>recalcitrant</u>. She seldom changes her mind.

___ 2. A <u>quotidian</u> event is a rare and unusual happening.

___ 3. When Jamie was offered a new position in Paris, she didn't accept it imme diately. She thought about it for a long time and talked it over with family and friends. She made a <u>rash</u> decision.

___ 4. The stock market took a downturn in February, but then it <u>rebounded</u> in March. This means that the stock market made up all its losses.

___ 5. One of his odd little <u>quirks</u> is that he will not step on a crack in the sidewalk.

___ 6. I couldn't get to sleep last night because my next door neighbors were hav- ing a <u>raucous</u> party.

___ 7. The crowd was <u>restive</u>. They were relaxed and calm.

___ 8. While that political movement is <u>quiescent</u> now, it may come roaring back to life at any time.

___ 9. "Don't <u>quibble</u> about the price" means don't argue or complain about how much something costs.

___ 10. The unexpected results of the experiment created a <u>quandary</u> for the researchers. They were confused and didn't know how to proceed.

Vocabulary Set 20: (*reticent* to *solemn*)

286. reticent Don't be <u>reticent</u>. If you know the answer, just shout it out!
part of speech _____ definition/synonyms _____
noun: **reticence**

287. rustic I don't want to spend my vacation in some <u>rustic</u> cabin in the mountains. I want to stay in a nice hotel on the beach.
part of speech _____ definition/synonyms _____

288. sage (adj) When I have a problem, I often go to my grandmother. She always has some <u>sage</u> advice for me.
part of speech _____ definition/synonyms _____
noun: **sagacity** agent noun: **sage**

289. salubrious In the past, patients who had tuberculosis were urged by doctors to move to a place with a dry climate. Places like Arizona or New Mexico were considered especially <u>salubrious</u>.
part of speech _____ definition/synonyms _____

290. sanguine Although his business is not doing very well now, he is <u>sanguine</u> about its future prospects.
part of speech _____ definition/synonyms _____

291. savvy This course is not meant for people who are already computer <u>savvy</u>; it's for people who are just learning computer basics.
part of speech _____ definition/synonyms _____
noun: **savvy**

292. scathing The newspaper published a <u>scathing</u> editorial about the mayor's recent policy decisions. It was also bitterly critical of the city council.
part of speech _____ definition/synonyms _____
adv: **scathingly**

293. scrutinize Unfortunately, I didn't <u>scrutinize</u> the contract carefully. I just gave it a cursory glance before I signed it.
part of speech _____ definition/synonyms _____
noun: **scrutiny**

294. **sedulous** He performed a <u>sedulous</u> search for the document, going through every folder in the old file cabinets.

part of speech _____ definition/synonyms _____

adv: **sedulously**

295. **shard** From just a few <u>shards</u> of broken pottery, the archaeologists were able to draw quite a few conclusions about the ancient civilization.

part of speech _____ definition/synonyms _____

296. **shrewd** Dusit's decision to buy that stock was a <u>shrewd</u> one. It tripled in value in less than a month.

part of speech _____ definition/synonyms _____

adv: **shrewdly**

297. **simulate** Film-makers often use computer-generated special effects to <u>simulate</u> scenes that would be expensive or dangerous to film, such as car crashes or explosions.

part of speech _____ definition/synonyms _____

noun: **simulation**

298. **sketchy** The information provided by eye-witnesses is often <u>sketchy</u>, providing few useful details.

part of speech _____ definition/synonyms _____

299. **solicitous** The nurse was quite <u>solicitous</u>, making sure that the patient was comfortable and not in any pain.

part of speech _____ definition/synonyms _____

300. **somber** The state funeral held for the queen was quite a <u>somber</u> affair.

part of speech _____ definition/synonyms _____

Vocabulary Exercise 20: Word Search

Find 12 words from Vocabulary Set 20 in the grid below. (The words in the list below are synonyms of the hidden words, not the words themselves.) The words in the grid can go in different directions: → (side-to-side, left to right), ↓ (down), ↘ (diagonal down, left to right), or ↗ (diagonal up, left to right).

When you have found the words from Set 20, write the word next to its synonyms. Then write the number of the vertical column in which the word begins (1-15), the number of the horizontal column in which the word begins (1-15), and the direction of the word (→ , ↓, ↘, or ↗). The first one is done as an example.

Word Starts in vertical column # Starts in horizontal row # Direction

1. to imitate; pretend; fake _simulate_   1   2   ↓

2. healthy; wholesome _____

3. fragment; broken piece _____

4. rural; in the countryside _____

5. scornful; bitter; caustic _____

6. vague; unclear; without details _____

7. clever; savvy; smart _____

8. shy; reserved; quiet _____

9. kind; considerate; helpful _____

10. to examine carefully; inspect _____

11. sad; gloomy; solemn _____

12. cheerful; optimistic _____

13. wise; intelligent _____

	1	2	3	4	5	6	7	8	9	10	11	12	12	14
1	F	U	Y	P	H	T	R	V	B	I	M	W	P	Y	V
2	S	P	S	I	O	W	U	G	Q	O	P	L	B	D	R
3	I	A	O	R	Z	I	S	K	E	T	C	H	Y	W	M
4	M	A	L	B	N	X	T	S	T	O	L	K	L	O	E
5	U	R	I	U	L	A	I	R	S	C	B	Y	V	G	X
6	L	C	C	D	B	S	C	O	R	P	O	M	A	N	T
7	A	E	I	S	H	R	E	W	D	F	L	S	E	D	O
8	T	U	T	I	E	E	I	N	E	G	R	C	R	V	R
9	E	D	O	J	B	T	B	O	R	O	U	A	G	I	Q
10	C	Q	U	E	N	I	N	G	U	W	H	T	K	L	S
11	L	I	S	F	J	C	T	Y	A	S	Y	H	F	R	O
12	Z	E	R	T	A	E	S	A	N	G	U	I	N	E	M
13	I	O	P	A	D	N	V	E	N	I	S	N	A	J	B
14	O	S	C	R	U	T	I	N	I	Z	E	G	I	D	E
15	W	X	L	T	A	R	J	S	T	E	V	A	N	O	R

Crossword Puzzle 5: Sets 17-20 (*parched* to *somber*)

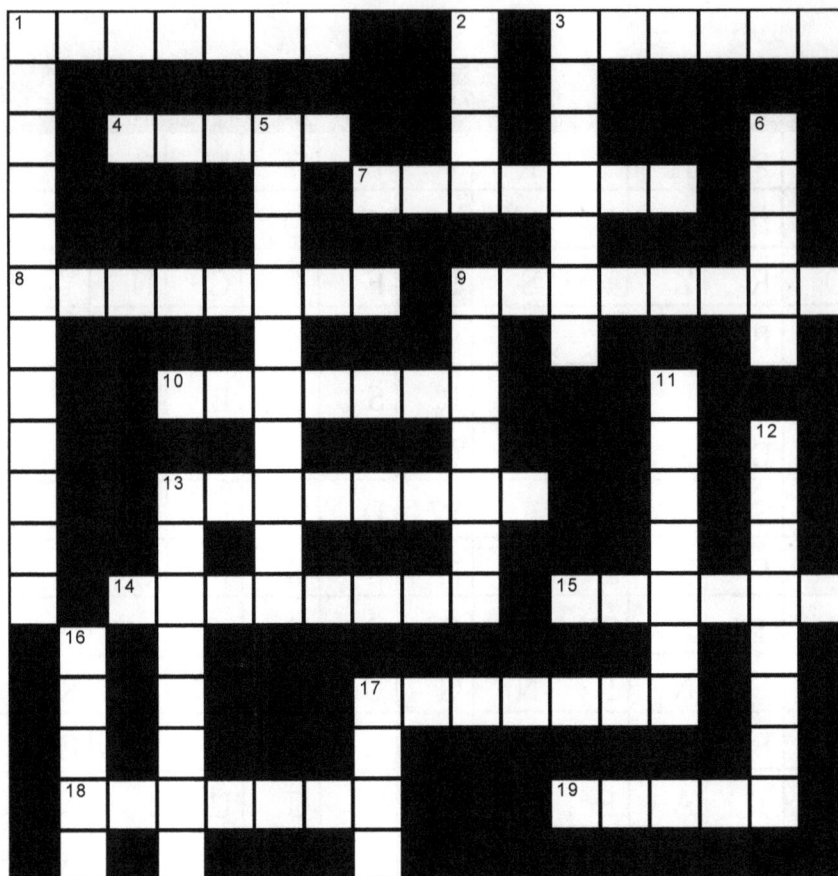

Across

1 Having a strong, acrid smell or taste
3 Wordy; verbose; speaking or writing too much
4 Luxurious; lavish; rich
7 Vague; unclear; not showing any details
8 Optimistic; confident; hopeful; upbeat; having a rosy outlook
9 Abundance; excess; having a large number or amount; superfluity
10 To squabble; argue about minor points
13 Creating a lot of something, especially art, music, or literature
14 Unspoiled; undeveloped; untouched
15 Old-fashioned in a charming way
17 Restless; uneasy; anxious; troubled
18 Loud; harsh; disorderly
19 Used to describe a brief but forceful statement; concise; terse

Down

1 Absurd; ludicrous; ridiculous
2 Wise; erudite; astute; clever
3 Desiccated; dehydrated; completely dry
5 Kind; helpful; caring; attentive
6 An unusual habit or behavior
9 Childish; immature; juvenile; foolish
11 Soothe; calm; mollify; appease; assuage
12 Dilemma; a difficult, confusing choice
13 Dangerous; hazardous; risky
16 A broken piece; a sliver; a chip
17 Hasty; careless; sudden; precipitate

Vocabulary Set 21: (*sonorous* to *tangible*)

---

301. **sonorous** The actor James Earl Jones has a deep, rich, <u>sonorous</u> voice. He often performs as a voice-over talent.
part of speech _____ definition/synonyms _____

---

302. **soporific** The professor's <u>soporific</u> lecture almost put the students to sleep.
part of speech _____ definition/synonyms _____

---

303. **sporadic** When the storm began, the crash of thunder was almost continuous, then it became <u>sporadic</u>, then finally it died out altogether.
part of speech _____ definition/synonyms _____

---

304. **specious** At first, many of us were convinced by his argument, but then we realized that it was completely <u>specious</u>.
part of speech _____ definition/synonyms _____

---

305. **spurious** Many photographs have been taken of Scotland's Loch Ness Monster, but so far, all of these images have been proven to be <u>spurious</u>. The monster in one of the most famous photos, taken in 1934, consisted of a toy submarine and a rubber model of the monster's head and neck.
part of speech _____ definition/synonyms _____

---

306. **spurn** Marcia <u>spurned</u> Rob's proposal to marry her. She said that she wouldn't marry him if he were the last man on earth.
part of speech _____ definition/synonyms _____

---

307. **squabble** Dominique told her two boys to stop <u>squabbling</u>. She said she was sick of hearing them bicker about whose toy that was.
part of speech _____ definition/synonyms _____

---

308. **squander** Jack has a good job but he never seems to have much money. He must be <u>squandering</u> his income on something.
part of speech _____ definition/synonyms _____

---

309. **stimulate** The central bank is trying to use monetary policy to <u>stimulate</u> the economy.
part of speech _____ definition/synonyms _____
noun: **stimulation** -ing adj: **stimulating**

---

310. **subtle** The forged painting looked to most people exactly like the genuine painting, but the expert could detect some <u>subtle</u> differences.
part of speech _____ definition/synonyms _____

311. **sumptuous** On Thanksgiving Day in the United States, most families sit down to a <u>sumptuous</u>, festive meal.
part of speech _____ definition/synonyms _____

312. **taciturn** Gustav was the driver of a tour bus, and he spent all day talking to tourists. Now he's retired, however, and he's become quite <u>taciturn</u>.
part of speech _____ definition/synonyms _____

313. (in) **tandem** James Watson, in <u>tandem</u> with Frances Crick, determined the double-helix structure of DNA.
part of speech _____ definition/synonyms _____

314. **tangential** We need to concentrate on the main topic and spend less time speaking of <u>tangential</u> issues.
part of speech _____ definition/synonyms _____
noun: **tangent**

315. **tangible** <u>Tangible</u> assists are things that one can actually see or touch. For example, if you are selling a restaurant, your oven and your tables and chairs would be <u>tangible</u> assets. If your restaurant has a good reputation, however, that would be an <u>intangible</u> asset.
part of speech _____ definition/synonyms _____
neg. adj: **intangible**

Vocabulary Exercise 21: Sentence Completion

Underline one of the two words in parentheses to create a logical sentence.

1. The explorers had heard rumors that there was a lost city hidden in the jungle, but they had no (tangible/tangential) evidence that it actually existed.

2. He (squabbled/squandered) a great opportunity.

3. Gregorio is not as talkative as he used to be. In fact, some days he's actually rather (subtle/taciturn).

4. She was listening intently to a recording of opera singer Elio Pinza's (sonorous/soporific) voice.

5. Rosalyn never wears strong perfumes–just a dab of a (subtle/tangible) floral scent.

6. Several scientists have claimed to have developed cold fusion as an energy source, but their claims have all turned out to be (specious/sporadic).

7. I expected we would just have a little snack on our hike, but my friends had put together a (spurious/ sumptuous) picnic lunch.

8. He's having problems in his math class, but he (spurned/squabbled) his teacher's offer to help him.

9. The government, working (in tandem/sporadically) with some private agencies, is trying to provide temporary housing for the people whose homes were damaged in the hurricane.

10. I find Dr. Nguyen's public lectures really (stimulating/soporific). She has some fascinating ideas about the future of medicine.

Vocabulary Set 22: (*tarnish* to *turbulent*)

---

316. **tarnish** Mr. Trigo's reputation was <u>tarnished</u> by the accusation that he had defrauded the public.

part of speech _____ definition/synonyms _____

-ed adj: **tarnished** neg -ed adj: **untarnished**

---

317. **tenet** Two of the generally accepted <u>tenets</u> of the modern cell theory are the idea that all living things are made up of cells, and that all cells come from the division of pre-existing cells.

part of speech _____ definition/synonyms _____

---

318. **tenuous** I have a <u>tenuous</u> grasp of some of the principles of calculus, but not a deep understanding of them.

part of speech _____ definition/synonyms _____

---

319. **tepid** The critics' response to the new television comedy "Family Tree" has been <u>tepid</u>, but it is quite popular with the viewing public.

part of speech _____ definition/synonyms _____

---

320. **terse** He emailed me a <u>terse</u> response to my request. It simply said, "Sorry, no."

part of speech _____ definition/synonyms _____

---

321. **thrifty** I love going to the Farmers' Market on Saturday. The fruits and vegetables are always fresh, and I just enjoy being there. However, it is not exactly a <u>thrifty</u> place to shop.

part of speech _____ definition/synonyms _____

noun: **thrift**

---

322. **thwart** The intruders' plan to steal those sensitive files was <u>thwarted</u> by an alert night watchman.

part of speech _____ definition/synonyms _____

---

323. **tirade** If you mention microwave ovens to Alicia, she will launch into a long <u>tirade</u> about why she thinks they are dangerous to your health.

part of speech _____ definition/synonyms _____

---

324. **topple** The cell-phone tower was <u>toppled</u> by the high winds last night.

part of speech _____ definition/synonyms _____

---

325. **torpor** On chilly nights, hummingbirds enter a state called <u>torpor</u>. They lock their feet onto a branch, lower their body temperature, and reduce their normally rapid heart rate to just a few beats per minute.
part of speech _____ definition/synonyms _____
adj. **torpid**

326. **tortuous** Neither a <u>tortuous</u> path nor a <u>tortuous</u> argument is easy to follow.
part of speech _____ definition/synonyms _____

327. **transitory** Occasionally, people studying the Moon with a telescope have seen brief flashes of light, which are called "<u>transitory</u> lunar phenomena," or TLPs.
part of speech _____ definition/synonyms _____

328. **trenchant** Expecting a compliment, Eleanor was stung by her sister's <u>trenchant</u> comment.
part of speech _____ definition/synonyms _____

329. **trite** Shakespeare's character Polonius, the advisor to the king in the play *Hamlet*, often gives advice. Some of his advice seems sage, some of it sounds rather <u>trite</u>.
part of speech _____ definition/synonyms _____

331. **truculent** Having lost the election, the candidate became <u>truculent</u>. In his concession speech, rather than wishing his opponent well, he bitterly criticized her as well as the voters who had rejected him.
part of speech _____ definition/synonyms _____
noun: **truculence** adv: **truculently**

Vocabulary Exercise 22: Matching

Match these words with their synonyms.

1. tortuous ___   A. principle; rule; guideline; maxim; dogma

2. torpor ___   B. to prevent something from happening; forestall

3. thrifty ___   C. to knock over; collapse; overthrow

4. tenet ___   D. a long, angry speech; harangue; diatribe

5. truculent ___   E. brief; temporary; fleeting; momentary

6. transitory ___   F. hostile; argumentative; belligerent; aggressive; fractious

7. trite ___   G. lethargy; laziness; languor; indolence; inactivity

8. thwart ___   H. commonplace; banal; ordinary; hackneyed; stale; mundane

9. trenchant ___   I. lukewarm; neither hot nor cold; unenthusiastic

10. tirade ___   J. wandering; indirect; meandering; having many twists and turns

11. topple ___   K. frugal; economical; careful with money

12. tepid ___   L. incisive; cutting; acerbic

Vocabulary Set 23: (*truculent* to *vindicate*)

---

330. **turbulent** The 1930s was a <u>turbulent</u> period in European history. The poet W. H. Auden called that time "a low, dark, dishonest decade."
part of speech _____ definition/synonyms _____
noun: **turbulence**

---

332. **tyro** The newly-hired pilot trainee is far from being a <u>tyro</u>. She has logged over two hundred hours of flight time as the first officer of an airliner.
part of speech _____ definition/synonyms _____

---

333. **ubiquitous** The first Starbuck's coffee shop opened in Seattle's Pike Place Market in 1971. Today, Starbucks are virtually <u>ubiquitous</u>. In some downtown areas, there is one on nearly every block.
part of speech _____ definition/synonyms _____
noun: **ubiquity**

---

334. **uncouth** My mother couldn't decide whether to invite Uncle Luke to the holiday party. She said that sometimes he acts <u>uncouth</u> at family gatherings.
part of speech _____ definition/synonyms _____

---

335. **unsullied** Sven got some pasta sauce on his tie, but at least his white shirt was <u>unsullied</u>.
part of speech _____ definition/synonyms _____

---

336. **upbraid** His parents <u>upbraided</u> him for missing so many classes.
part of speech _____ definition/synonyms _____

---

337. **urbane** In high school, Nicolas was not very sophisticated, but after four years of college, he's become quite an <u>urbane</u> young man.
part of speech _____ definition/synonyms _____

---

338. **vacillate** Who knows what he will finally decide? He keeps <u>vacillating</u>.
part of speech _____ definition/synonyms _____
noun: **vacillation**

---

339. **vapid** My roommate likes reality TV shows, but I find them quite <u>vapid</u>. I have to go into the other room when she watches them
part of speech _____ definition/synonyms _____

---

340. **veracious** We had a hard time deciding whether he was being <u>veracious</u> or if he was making the entire story up.

part of speech _____ definition/synonyms _____

noun: **veracity**

341. **verbose** The best advice I ever got from my public speaking teacher was to avoid being <u>verbose</u>. "Never use two words when one word will do," he used to tell the class.

part of speech _____ definition/synonyms _____

noun: **verbosity**

342. **versatile** The Swiss Army knife is a <u>versatile</u> tool.

part of speech _____ definition/synonyms _____

noun: **versatility**

343. **vex** A lack of parking places is a <u>vexing</u> problem in most big cities.

part of speech _____ definition/synonyms _____

-ing adj: **vexing**

344. **vie** In the nineteenth century, the competition between railroads that followed the same routes was intense. In fact, to <u>vie</u> for passengers, some railroads cut ticket prices so much that the railroads actually lost money on every trip.

part of speech _____ definition/synonyms _____

345. **vindicate** At first, many scientists criticized Professor Chopra's findings. However, recent studies showed that his claims were accurate, and he now feels <u>vindicated</u>.

part of speech _____ definition/synonyms _____

noun: **vindication**

Vocabulary Exercise 23: Similar Sentences

If the two sentences have similar meanings, mark them **S**. If they have different meanings, mark them **X**.

____ 1.   A. There are nearly 10,000 applicants <u>vying</u> for admission to this MBA program, but only about 12% are accepted.
        B. The competition for admission to this business school is fierce.

____ 2.   A I believe he was completely <u>veracious</u>.
        B. I think he was really hungry.

____ 3.   A. Amelie is stylish and <u>urbane</u>.
        B. She is fashionable and she lives in a big city.

____ 4.   A. Crystal Canyon is still a pristine area.
        B. The canyon is <u>unsullied</u> so far.

____ 5.   A. Su-Mee can play the violin, the piano, the flute, and several other instruments.
        B. Su-Mee is a <u>versatile</u> musician.

____ 6.   A. Theresa said she found the book <u>vapid</u>.
        B. She said it was clear and easy to read.

____ 7.   A. The two countries have long had a <u>turbulent</u> relationship.
        B. For many years, the two nations have been close allies.

____ 8.   A. Amber warned her boyfriend not to be boorish.
        B. She told him not to be <u>uncouth</u>.

____ 9.   A. He was upset that he had to sit in the waiting room for so long.
        B. He was <u>vexed</u> by the long delay.

____ 10. A. When it comes to playing online games, I'm a <u>tyro</u>.
        B. I don't have much experience playing online games.

Vocabulary Set 24: (*viscous* to *zealous*)

---

346. **viscous** Honey and motor oil are both <u>viscous</u> liquids.
part of speech _____   definition/synonyms _____
noun: **viscosity**

---

347. **vituperative** The editor of the blog decided to eliminate the online comments section because so many of the comments had a <u>vituperative</u> tone.
part of speech _____   definition/synonyms _____

---

348. **vivacious**   The people I used to work with were <u>vivacious</u> and fun to be around. Since I changed jobs, though, my co-workers are far more serious and want to talk only about business.
part of speech _____   definition/synonyms _____

---

349. **voracious** My little brother has a <u>voracious</u> appetite. Last night he ordered two large pizzas just for himself.
part of speech _____   definition/synonyms _____

---

350. **wane** At first he had a lot of enthusiasm for this project, but after a few disappointing set-backs, his enthusiasm began to <u>wane</u>.
part of speech _____   definition/synonyms _____
-ing adj: **waning**

---

351. **wary** Anytime an offer seems too good to be true, be <u>wary</u>. It probably *is* too good to be true.
part of speech _____   definition/synonyms _____
noun: **wariness** adv: **warily**

---

352. **waver**   His belief that his invention would eventually be successful never <u>wavered</u>.
part of speech _____   definition/synonyms _____

---

353. **whimsical** Selena was <u>whimsical</u> as a teenager, but she has become much more serious and practical.
part of speech _____   definition/synonyms _____
nouns: **whim, whimsy** adv: **whimsically**

---

354. **wince** Harvey <u>winced</u> when he hit his thumb with a hammer.
part of speech _____   definition/synonyms _____

---

355. **wishy-washy** Don't be so <u>wishy-washy</u>! Make up your mind!
part of speech _____ definition/synonyms _____

356. **wistful** Whenever she speaks of her childhood friends, her voice takes on a <u>wistful</u> tone.
part of speech _____ definition/synonyms _____

357. **woe** Dorothea Lange's photos, taken during the Great Depression of the 1930s, perfectly illustrate the <u>woes</u> of migrant farm workers and the rural poor.
part of speech _____ definition/synonyms _____
adj: **woeful**

358. **woo** Male bower birds build elaborate structures and decorate them with sticks and brightly colored objects in order to <u>woo</u> female bower birds.
part of speech _____ definition/synonyms _____

359. **wretched** I had a <u>wretched</u> flight from London to New York. First, we sat on the runway for three hours before taking off. Then we ran into some really bad turbulence. And finally, there were two or three babies sitting near me who cried for much of the trip.
part of speech _____ definition/synonyms _____

360. **zealous** Patrick Henry was a <u>zealous</u> supporter of American independence. He once said, "Give me liberty or give me death."
part of speech _____ definition/synonyms _____
adv: **zealously** noun: **zeal** agent noun: **zealot**

Vocabulary Exercise 24: Error Check

If the sentences below are true or logical, mark them **YES**. If the sentences are false or illogical, mark them **NO**.

____ 1. When the moon begins to <u>wane</u>, it appears to get larger every night.

____ 2. <u>Wishy-washy</u> people are irresolute.

____ 3. <u>Zealous</u> people are apathetic.

____ 5. Patrice <u>winced</u> when he heard the good news.

____ 4. The governor is trying to <u>woo</u> a European automaker to open a factory in her state by offering the automotive company tax breaks and other benefits.

____ 6. Many liquids become more <u>viscous</u> when the weather is cold.

____ 7. If you go into the swamp, be <u>wary</u> of snakes and alligators.

____ 8. A <u>voracious</u> person is always truthful.

____ 9. Sherry has a <u>vivacious</u> personality. In other words, she is ebullient and high-spirited.

____ 10. "He didn't <u>waver</u> in his belief" means that he never changed his mind.

Crossword Puzzle 6: Sets 21-24 (*sonorous* to *zealous*)

Across

1 Thick; sticky, like syrup or honey
3 Sad; melancholy; pensive; nostalgic
6 Lukewarm; not warm and not cold; unenthusiastic
8 Sophisticated; polished; suave; elegant
10 Encourage; incite; goad; get moving
12 Enthusiastic; ardent; fervent
14 Quiet; laconic; not talkative
16 Novice; fledgling; beginner
17 Having a rich, powerful voice
20 Careful; alert; watchful
21 To argue about minor points; quibble; bicker
22 To have an expression that shows momentary pain

Down

2 Making someone feel sleepy; boring
3 A problem; something that causes sorrow or distress; a trouble
4 Intermittent; happening on and off; desultory
5 Boorish; crude; rude; unmannered; impolite
6 Pithy; brief; succinct; precise
7 To diminish; decrease; shrink; dwindle
9 Plush; luxurious; opulent; lavish
11 Temporary; momentary; short-lived
13 Twisting; meandering; indirect; convoluted
15 Perceptible; touchable; palpable; actual; real
16 To prevent; counter; forestall
18 To reject; refuse; treat with scorn
19 To compete; to challenge
20 To try to attract; to court

Vocabulary Review I: Sets 1-30

Odd One Out

Cross out the word in each group that does NOT belong with the other words. The first one has been done as an example.

1.	paucity	dearth	~~shard~~	scarcity	
2.	garrulous	shrewd	loquacious	verbose	prolix
3.	mordant	complaisant	trenchant	caustic	acerbic
4.	relish	bicker	squabble	quibble	
5.	banal	mundane	pedestrian	lucrative	prosaic
6.	unsullied	pristine	disabused	undisturbed	
7.	capricious	whimsical	impulsive	conspicuous	
8.	laconic	taciturn	facetious	reticent	
9.	frugal	thrifty	feasible	economical	
10.	fatuous	recalcitrant	intractable	refractory	adamant
11.	apathetic lackadaisical	indifferent	arbitrary	unconcerned	nonchalant
12.	bolster	languish	buttress	support	
13.	appease pacify	mollify	assuage	allure	placate
14.	desultory	contentious	haphazard	random	
15.	mendacious	disingenuous	mercurial	dissembling	
16.	sedulous	meticulous	assiduous	diligent	felicitous
17.	tyro fledgling	neophyte	novice	miser	beginner
18.	mushrooming	baffling	burgeoning	expanding	
19.	obtuse	fatuous	silly	foolhardy	facetious
20.	tirade	harangue	diatribe	hiatus	
21.	moribund	esoteric	recondite	obscure	abstruse
22.	lethargy	jargon	lassitude	torpor	indolence
23.	fervent	austere	zealous	ardent	enthusiastic
24.	meandering	oblivious	convoluted	tortuous	
25.	precarious	perilous	risky	spurious	hazardous
26.	dissemble	disparage	prevaricate	lie	
27.	vituperative	acerbic	scathing	acrimonious	raucous

28.	enigma riddle	conundrum	puzzle	chicanery	mystery
29.	craven	destitute	indigent	impecunious	impoverished
30.	irresolute	peripheral	wishy-washy	vacillating	wavering
31.	contentious	affable	amiable	genial	cordial
32.	sage	erudite	astute	wary	ingenious
33.	drench	saturate	simulate	soak	inundate
34.	bland	insipid	vapid	solicitous	
35.	disparage	denigrate	disabuse	discredit	
36.	inept	feckless	charismatic	incompetent	
37.	irascible testy	impassivee	grumpy	petulant	grouchy
38.	plush	parched	desiccated	arid	dehydrated
39.	flamboyant	gaudy	ostentatious	rapacious	
40.	tangential	peripheral	pivotal	marginal	
41.	levity	frivolity	ambiguity	lightheartedness	
42.	appropriate	apt	fitting	bombastic	felicitous
43.	restive	unsettled	turbulent	quiescent	
44.	hamper	obstruct	topple	hinder	
45.	cursory	fleeting	hasty	wretched	rushed
46.	sketchy	malodorous	pungent	acrid	
47.	crude	copious	boorish	unmannered	uncouth
48.	plunge	drop	mar	nosedive	plummet
49.	spurious	false	specious	prescient	
50.	quotidian	humdrum	ordinary	gullible	mundane

Vocabulary Review II: Sets 1-36

Similar, Opposite, or Unrelated?

If the following pairs of words are synonyms or very close in meaning, mark them **S**. If they are antonyms (having opposite, or nearly opposite meanings) mark them **A**. If they are neither synonyms nor antonyms, mark them **X**. The first one has been done as an example.

1. _S_ wretched / execrable
2. ___ oblivious / subtle
3. ___ fleeting / transitory
4. ___ miserly / beneficent
5. ___ alleviate / exacerbate
6. ___ wince / quirk
7. ___ hasty / rash
8. ___ eclectic / disparate
9. ___ loquacious / taciturn
10. ___ sage / fatuous
11. ___ abate / mar
12. ___ plethora / myriad
13. ___ dwindle / mushroom
14. ___ amiable / truculent
15. ___ apathy / zeal
16. ___ viscous / nostalgic
17. ___ insipid / vapid
18. ___ assiduous / sedulous
19. ___ wane / burgeon
20. ___ lassitude / torpor
21. ___ vex / mollify
22. ___ tortuous / meandering
23. ___ fluke / hoax
24. ___ veracious / candid
25. ___ obdurate / fastidious
26. ___ querulous / petulant
27. ___ tirade / harangue
28. ___ dearth / plethora
29. ___ turbulent / quiescent
30. ___ craven / audacious
31. ___ ebullient / morose
32. ___ cacophonous / raucous
33. ___ pristine / unsullied
34. ___ enigma / conundrum
35. ___ trenchant / aloof
36. ___ vacillate / waver
37. ___ wary / savvy
38. ___ baffling / abstruse
39. ___ haphazard / perilous
40. ___ apt / felicitous
41. ___ vapid / hasty
42. ___ facetious / astute
43. ___ gullible / garrulous
44. ___ disingenuous / mendacious
45. ___ overt / clandestine
46. ___ ardent / fervent
47. ___ nonchalant / mediocre
48. ___ exotic / banal
49. ___ tarnish / burnish
50. ___ colossal / minute
51. ___ pungent / feasible
52. ___ woo / allure
53. ___ impassive / salubrious
54. ___ bolster / buttress
55. ___ flamboyant / gaudy
56. ___ approbation / castigation
57. ___ boorish / urbane
58. ___ tangible / palpable
59. ___ ephemeral / mercurial
60. ___ plush / sumptuous

Common English Word Roots

A root, as the name suggests, is a word or word-part from which other words grow, usually by adding prefixes and suffixes. Understanding common word roots can help you figure out the meanings of unfamiliar words that you encounter on the GRE. But be careful: word roots can have more than one meaning or can have various shades of meaning. Moreover, words that appear similar may derive from different roots.

The lists below contain some of the most common Greek and Latin roots. (Note: Some of the examples given are not likely to be tested on the exam.)

Words in *italics* appear in the list of "360 Common GRE Words" list.

Set 1

Word root	Meaning	Examples
-acr-, -acer-	sharp, bitter	*acrid*; *acerbic*
-agri-, -agro-, -agra-	field, farm	agronomy; agrarian
-ali-, -alter-	another, foreign	alias; alternate; alien
-alti-, -alt-	high	altimeter; alto
-am-, -amor-	love, friendship	amorous; amateur; *amiable*
-anthro-	person, human, male	anthropology; philanthropy
-aqua-, aqu-	water	aquarium; aquaculture; aqueduct
-arch-, -arc-	ruler, control	anarchy; autocracy; matriarch; patriarchy
-ast-, -aster-	star	astronaut; astronomy; asteroid; aster
-aud-	hear, sound	auditory; audition; inaudible
-auto-	self	automobile; automatic

Directions: Write a synonym or a brief definition of the underlined words in the sentences below. If you don't know the meaning of a word, make a guess based on the meaning of the word root.

1. In the Western U.S., over 80% of all water use is for _agricultural_ purposes.
   _____

2. The two countries settled their disagreement in an _amicable_ way.
   _____

3. He _alienated_ his friends and family with his angry attitude. _____

4. My Uncle Bill is not really a _misanthrope_, but he doesn't like socializing very much. _____

5. Some mollusks live on land while others are _aquatic_ animals. _____

6. My cousins had an _acrimonious_ discussion about the outcome of the election.
   _____

7. Queen Elizabeth I was the fifth and last _monarch_ of the Tudor dynasty.
   _____

8. The band will give a concert in the school _auditorium_. _____

9. Some the people's names on the list had _asterisks_ beside them—for example, Jennifer Evans*. _____

10. At one time, both the state of Texas and the state of California were _autonomous_ countries. _____

11. Denver is nicknamed the Mile High City because it is at an _altitude_ of 5,280 feet (one mile). _____

Set 2

Word root	Meaning	Examples
-belli-	war, fighting	belligerent; rebellious
-ben-	good	*beneficent*; benign
-bio-	life	biology; antibiotics
-brev-; -bridg-	short	brevity; abridged
-cap-, -capt-	head	captain; decapitate; capital; capitulate
-carn-	flesh, meat	carnage; carnival
-celer-	speed	celerity; decelerate
-chron-	time	chronic; anachronous; chronometer; chronicle
-cide-	kill	suicide; homicide; herbicide
-civi-	citizen	civilian; civilization; civil; civics
-cline-	lean; lean backwards	recline; incline; decline
-clud-, -clus-, -clos-, -claus-	shut, close	include; *preclude*; enclose; conclusive; closet; exclude; secluded; inclusive
-corp-	body	incorporate; corps; corporeal
-cred-	believe	incredible; credit; creditable; *discredit*; incredulous
-cur-, -cour-	run	current; occur; incur; precursor; cursory; discourse; curriculum; course; recur; excursive; succor

12. Some chemical <u>pestic*ides*</u> such as DDT have been banned in the US because they are harmful to birds and other animals. _____

13. Carl Sandberg wrote a famous <u>*bio*graphy</u> of Abraham Lincoln.
    _____

14. English still uses some Latin <u>*abbrev*iations</u>, such as e.g., which is short for the Latin phrase "exempli gratia." This phrase means "for example" in English.
    _____

15. If a report begins, "Let's first consider the most recent events," it is not in <u>*chron*ological</u> order. _____

16. Lions and tigers are <u>*carn*ivorous</u> animals. _____

17. That sports car can <u>*acceler*ate</u> from 0 to 60 miles per hour in a few seconds.
    _____

18. At first, everyone was <u>*incred*ulous</u> of Jane's story.
    _____

19. Geese can be <u>*belli*cose</u> birds. _____

20. Before the boat sank, it <u>*cap*sized</u>. _____

21. Knowing Greek and Latin roots can be <u>*bene*ficial</u> when learning English vocabulary. _____

22. Abbas was <u>disin*clined*</u> to follow those orders. _____

Set 3

Word root	Meaning	Examples
-demo-, -dem-	people	democracy; demographics; demagogue
-dict-	speak	dictionary; diction; dictator; dictate; indict; edict
-domes-, -dom-	home	domestic; domicile
-dom-	control; have power	dominion; dominate; predominate
-duc-, -duct-	lead; make	introduction; product; conduct; reduction
-dur-	last; continue; firm	duration; endure; *obdurate*; duress
-dyna-	power; energy	dynamite; dynamo
equa-, equi-	same	equal; equation; equalize; equanimity
-fac-	make; do	factory; manufacture
-fal-	deceive; be wrong	false; fallacious
-fer-	carry; bring; move	conference; infer; defer; transfer
-fin-	end; limit	final; finite; confine
-flam-	fire; flame	*flamboyant*; inflammatory; flammable
-flate-	blow; fill with air	inflate; deflate; *conflate*
-flex-, flect-, flu-, -flux-	bend; move; flow	flexible; inflection; reflex; influx; confluence; reflection; fluid
-for-, -fore-	in front of	forward; before; forearm; *forestall*; forewarn; forebears

23. The economist pre<u>dict</u>ed that oil prices would go down _____

24. Cats and dogs are *dom<u>es</u>ticated* animals. _____

25. Vince was accused of _falsifying_ the document. _____

26. Albert Einstein once wrote, "Only two things are _infinite_, the universe and human stupidity, and I have some doubts about the universe."
_____

27. The archaeologists found some ancient _artifacts_ that had been used by people thousands of years ago. _____

28. Automobiles, refrigerators, sewing machines, dining room funiture: these are all examples of what economists call _durable_ goods. _____

29. Winston Churchill was a very _dynamic_ speaker. _____

30. The ancient Greek language was quite a bit different from the _demotic_ Greek that is spoken today. _____

31. Ms. Kim tried to _induce_ me to take over her project. _____

32. Elspeth's boss is very _domineering_. _____

33. I speak a little Italian, but I don't speak it _fluently_. _____

34. New York City is about _equi_distant between Boston and Washington, D.C.
_____

35. Snow had been _forecast_ last night, but instead there was just a light rain.
_____

Set 4

Word root	Meaning	Examples
-form-	shape	formal; conform; deform; information; formless; uniform; transform; formation
-fort-	strong	fortify; fortification
-frag-, -fract-	break; piece	fragment; fraction; fractal; refraction; infraction
-fug	flee; run away	refuge; fugitive
-gen-	make; create	engender; progenitor; genesis; degenerate
-grad-, -gress-	step; go	digress; progress; graduate
-graph-, -gram-	write	graphic; grammar; telegraph
-greg-	group; flock	gregarious; aggregate
-hydr-	water	dehydrated; hydrology
-itin-	travel; march	itinerary
-jet-, -ject-	throw	jettison; eject; projectile; reject; interjection
-jur-, -jus-, -jud-	law	jury; justice; judge; justify; injustice; judicate; unjust; justifiable

36. The decision he made showed a lot of moral _fortitude_. _____

37. An angry crowd con<u>greg</u>ated in the central square. _____

38. The doctor gave him an in<u>ject</u>ion. _____

39. Nomads are _itin_erant people. _____

40. Dagmar _fract_ured her ankle in a skiing accident. _____

41. If you work out at the gym, you need to stay _hydrat_ed. _____

42. He's _gradually_ improving his vocabulary. _____

43. Wind and sunlight can be used to _generate_ electricity. _____

44. There was a _fugacious_ interest in that quiz show when it first came on the air, but it was canceled after the first season. _____

45. The US government is divided into three branches: executive, legislative, and _judicial_. _____

Set 5

Word root	Meaning	Examples
-labor-	work	laboratory; elaborate; laborious
-laud-	praise	laud; applaud
-lect-	read; choose	elect; selection; lecture
-leg-	law	legality; legislate; illegal
-lev-, -lieve-	lift; light weight	*levity*; elevate; relieve; leverage
-liber-	free	liberate; liberal; liberator; illiberal
-liter-	letters	literature; alliterative; literate
-log-	study	psychology; biological; logical
-loq-, -loc-	speak	elocution; soliloquy; interlocution ; grandiloquent
-luc-, -lum-	light	*luminous*; *lucid*; illuminate; pellucid; elucidate

46. Too many people in my country are il*liter*ate. _____

47. Madison is getting her master's degree in zoo*logy*. _____

48. My colleague and I col*labor*ated on this project. _____

49. The city government is taking steps to al*lev*iate the problem of traffic congestion. _____

50. The national motto of France is "*Liber*ty, equality, and fraternity." _____

51. The glass was <u>translucent</u> but not transparent. _____

52. Congress is the <u>legislative</u> branch of government in the United States.
    _____

53. John F. Kennedy and Martin Luther King were <u>eloquent</u> speakers.

    _____

Set 6

Word root	Meaning	Examples
-magn-	great	magnanimous; magnify; magnate; magnitude
-mal-	bad	maleficent; *malodorous*; malady; malfunction; maladjusted; malicious; malpractice
-manu-	hand	manuscript; manufacture
-mari-	sea	marina; submarine
-mel-	sweet	ameliorate; melody
-min-, -mini-	small. make smaller	minor; diminutive; minute; miniscule; minimum; minority; diminish; miniature
-mis-, -mit-	send	missile; remit; transmit; missive
-mon-, -mono-	one; single	monarchy; monopoly
-morph-	form; shape	morphology; amorphous
-mut-, -muta-	change	mutate; transmute

54. Nova Scotia, New Brunswick, and Prince Edward Island: these are Canada's _mari_time provinces. _____

55. That star _emits_ a strange form of radiation. _____

56. The law of gravity is imm_utable_. _____

57. The robot spoke in a _mono_tone. _____

58. She has a _mel_lifluous singing voice. _____

59. Some insects undergo meta_morphosis_. _____

60. He began as a _man_ual worker, but he became president of a construction company._____

61. Meryl Streep's performance in that movie was *magnificent*.

   _____

62. Scurvy is a form of *malnutrition* caused by a lack of vitamin C.

   _____

Set 7

Word root	Meaning	Examples
-nat-, -nasc-	birth; come from	native; nascent; natural; nation
-nav-	sail; ship	navy; naval
-nomen-, -nomin-, -non-; -nym-	name	nomenclature; denomination; anonymous; synonym; homonym; nominee
-nov-	new	novel; innovate; novice; nova
-omni-	all	omnipotent; omniscient
-oper-	work	operation; cooperate; opera
-pac-, -plac-	peace	*pacify*; implacable; *placate*
- path-, -pass-	feeling; disease	pathology; pathetic; apathy; empathetic; passion; *impassive*
-ped-, -pod-, -pied-	foot	impede; *pedestrian*; podiatrist; pedal; biped; piedmont
-pel-, -pul-	push; drive; move	impel; compulsive; repel; pulsate; repulsive; *impulsive*; pulse

63. A sextant is an instrument used in _navigation_. _____

64. The president _nominated_ Judge Fisher to be a federal judge. _____

65. She had few _innate_ abilities as an athlete; she simply worked and trained hard. _____

66. The elevator is still _inoperable_. _____

67. They purchased supplies and equipment for their _expedition_._____

68. Some cows were grazing _placidly_ in the pasture. _____

69. The couple plans to <u>renovate</u> their kitchen themselves. _____

70. Bears are <u>*omnivorous*</u> animals. _____

71. The politician claimed to have a great deal of <u>em*pathy* </u> for the unemployed, but in reality, he did very little to help them. _____

Set 8

Word root	Meaning	Examples
-pen-	punish	penitent; penance; repent
-pend-	hang; weight; attach	pendant; dependent; suspend; independence; compendium
-phon-	voice; sound	symphony; euphonious; phonics; *cacophonous*
-photo-	light	photograph; photosynthesis
-pol-	city	metropolis; police; political; policy; cosmopolitan
-pon-, -pos-	place; put	postpone; opponent; exposition; propose; position; posture; impose
-pop-	people	popular; population
-port-	carry; bring	portable; export; report; transportation; portal
-pot-, -poten-	able; powerful	potential; impotent; potentate
-prim-	first	prime; primary; primal; primacy
-prox-	close; near	proximity; approximate
-psych-	mind	psychological; psychic; psychopath
-pug-, -pugn-	fight; strike	pugilist; oppugn; repugnant; impugn
-punc-	point; dot; mark	punctual; puncture

72. Ms. Romero imports tropical fruits: mangos, papayas, and pineapples.

   _____

73. English is not a *phonetic* language, but Spanish is. _____

74. Cecil was in a *pugnacious* mood. _____

75. Penicillin is a _potent_ antibiotic. _____

76. As Mexico City grew in size, it became a _megalapolis_. _____

77. Alcatraz, a former _penitentiary_, is located on a small island in San Francisco Bay. _____

78. Amparo is extremely _photogenic_. No wonder she wants to be a model. _____

79. The Indonesian archipelago consists of around 18,000 islands; all but about 1,000 are _unpopulated_. _____

80. Schizophrenia is a form of _psychosis_. _____

81. King Louis XVI was _deposed_ during the French Revolution. _____

82. Alison bought that dress on a sudden _impulse_. _____

83. When I told my sister that I'd had to cancel my trip, she didn't seem very _sympathetic_. _____

84. The _punctuation_ mark known as a period (.) in the US is called a full-stop in the UK. _____

85. Personal computers from the 1980s may seem _primitive_ to us today, but they were the forerunners of the computer revolution. _____

86. You'll find this information in the _appendix_ of the book. _____

Set 9

Word root	Meaning	Examples
-quir-, -quis-, -ques-, -quer-	ask; look for	inquiry; inquest; request; quest; question; query; quiz
-reg-, -rect-	straight	regular; regimen; regulate; rectangle; correct; direct; rectitude
-ri-, -rid-, -ris-	laugh	ridiculous; deride
-roga-,	ask; question; presume	interrogate; arrogant; derogatory
-rupt-	break	interrupt; disruptive; abrupt
-salv-, sal-	save; health	*salubrious*; salvation; salve
-scend-, -scent-	climb	ascend; ascendant; descendent
-sci-	know	science; conscious; omniscient; conscientious
-scrib-, -script-	write	scribe; scribble; transcribe; prescription; describe; script; proscribe; inscription
-sect-	cut	section; sector; intersect
-sed-, sess-, -sid-	sit	sediment; session; possess; reside; sessile

87. The novels of Jules Verne and H. G. Wells, though written long ago, are quite <u>pre*sci*ent</u>. _____

88. The ship sank, but its cargo could be <u>*salv*aged</u>. _____

89. What is an <u>interro*ga*tive</u> sentence? _____

90. Race cars have special gas tanks that are hard to <u>*rupt*ure</u> in case of an accident. _____

91. The weary climbers <u>de*scend*ed</u> the mountain. _____

92. The author's <u>manuscript</u> was rejected several times before it was accepted and became a best-seller. _____

93. All scientists should be <u>inquisitive</u>. _____

94. In my high-school biology class, we <u>dissected</u> a frog. _____

95. His teacher helped him <u>rectify</u> the mistakes in his essay. _____

96. Martin's solution to the problem was <u>risible</u>. _____

97. "Couch potato" is a disparaging term for a <u>sedentary</u> person. _____

Set 10

Word root	Meaning	Examples
-sens-, -sent-	feel; be aware	sensitive; sentiment; consent; dissent
-sequ-, -secu-, -sue-	follow	sequence; consecutive; pursue
-sim-, -simul-	same	similar; assimilate; simultaneous; facsimile; veri-similitude
-son-	sound	sonic; *sonorous*; resonate; song; dissonant; assonance
-sol-	alone	solitude; desolate; absolute
-solv-, -solu-	loosen	solve; dissolve, solution; resolve
-soph-	wisdom; knowledge	philosophy; sophomore; sophistry
-spect-, -spic-	see; look at	inspect; retrospective; prospect; spectacles; expect; *conspicuous*; specimen; introspection; spectrum; speculate
-spir-,	breath; spirit; soul	spiritual; conspire; respiration; expire; perspire; aspire
-stat-	stand; position	statue; stationary; station; stature
-strict-, string-	draw tight	strict; stricture; restrict; stringent

98. Natasha has very <u>soph</u>isticated taste in music and art. _____

99. In the Victorian era, women's clothing was quite con<u>strict</u>ive. _____

100. His <u>stat</u>us in class improved after he won that award. _____

101. It was a <u>spect</u>acular fireworks display. _____

102. Charles Lindberg made the first <u>sol</u>o flight across the Atlantic. _____

103. The Beatles' music in<u>spir</u>ed many other musicians. _____

104. Much of San Francisco was destroyed in the 1906 earthquake and by the subsequent fires. _____

105. Anesthesia makes patients insensible to pain. _____

106. "Her new sports car is as fast as lighting." This is a simile. _____

107. Water is sometimes called "the universal solvent." _____

Set 11

Word root	Meaning	Examples
-tact-, -tang-, tag-, -tig-	touch	tactile; tangent; *tangential*; intangible; contagious
-temp-	time	temporary; tempo; extemporaneous
-ten-, -tend-, -tain-	hold	tenant; untenable; detention; contain; abstain; extend; tendency; distend; maintain; retain; intend
-terra-	earth	terrain; territory; subterranean
-therm-	heat	thermometer; thermos; thermostat
-tract-	pull; draw	tractor; attract; subtract; distract; contract; tractable
-turb-; -tur-	spin around; confuse	disturb; perturb; turbid; turbulence
-uni-, -un-	one	unity; universal; university; uniform; unicorn
-urb-	city	urban; *urbane*; suburban

108. When the president announced an end to the subsidies on basic foods and fuel, there was <u>tur</u>moil in the streets of the capital. _____

109. Sometimes an external threat can <u>unif</u>y a group. _____

110. The *Independence Day* movies were about <u>extraterre</u>strial invasions. _____

111. The Renaissance artists Michelangelo and Leonardo da Vinci were <u>con<i>temp</i>o</u>raries. _____

112. Matt is a very <u>in<i>tract</i></u>able child. _____

113. Iceland is one of the biggest users of <u>geo<i>therm</i>a</u>l energy. _____

114. The director realized that his position had become <u>untenable,</u> and he resigned.

    _____

115. He arrived on an <u>interurban</u> train. _____

116. There are 48 <u>contiguous</u> states in the United States. _____

Set 12

Word root	Meaning	Examples
-vac-	empty	vacation; vacuum; evacuate
-ver-	truth	veracity; *veracious*; aver; very
-vert-, -vers-	turn	*divert*; invert; avert; convert; conversion; revert; controversy; versatile; reverse; averse; *versatile*; introverted; irreversible; *inadvertent*; obverse
-verb-	word	verb; verbal; reverberate; *verbose*
-vict-, -vinc-	conquer	victory; evict; convict
-vita-, -viva-, -viv-, -vig-	life; health	vitamin; vital; vitality; vivid; survive; *vivacious*; vigor; *invigorate*; vigorous
-vid-, -vis-	see	video; vision, invisible; television; visit
-voc-; -vok-	call; speak	vocation; evoke; invoke; provoke; vocalize; vocabulary; revoke
-vor-	eat	*voracious*; carnivore; herbivore

117. Sheep and goats are herbi<u>vor</u>ous animals. _____

118. The activists were making <u>voc</u>iferous demands. _____

119. Some large animal must have recently <u>vac</u>ated this cave. _____

120. The report couldn't be <u>ver</u>ified. _____

121. The child was too young to <u>verb</u>alize her worries. _____

122. The flight from Frankfurt to Boston was di<u>vert</u>ed to an airport in Canada be cause of a mechanical problem on board the plane. _____

123. Everyone thought the team was in<u>vinc</u>ible, but they lost the first game of the season. _____

124. If you climb to the top of this hill, you'll see a beautiful _vista_. _____

125. The surgeon was able to _revive_ the patient. _____

Supplemental Vocabulary List

Many of the following 400 words have appeared on past GRE exams. Others are likely to appear on exams in the future.

1. abashed
2. abet
3. abhor
4. abrasive
5. abridged
6. abstemious
7. acclaim
8. accolades
9. acquiesce
10. advocate
11. affluent
12. aftermath
13. aghast
14. agile
15. akin (to)
16. alienate
17. allege
18. ameliorate
19. amenity
20. anachronous
21. analogous
22. anathema
23. anecdotal
24. antedate
25. apex
26. apocryphal
27. appalling
28. apparatus
29. apposite
30. arcane
31. articulate
32. aspire
33. assimilate
34. augment

35. autochthonous
36. avaricious
37. aver
38. averse
39. awry
40. badger (v.)
41. balmy
42. banter
43. begrudge
44. belittle
45. bellicose
46. bequeath
47. berate
48. beseech
49. blatant
50. blinkered
51. blunder
52. bogus
53. boisterous
54. boom
55. boon
56. brusque
57. bucolic
58. budding
59. bulging
60. bungle
61. burdensome
62. cajole
63. callous
64. callow
65. calumny
66. cantankerous
67. capacious
68. captious

108. dank
109. debilitating
110. debunk
111. decry
112. deface
113. defame
114. defraud
115. degrade
116. demur
117. demure
118. descry
119. deter
120. didactic
121. dilapidated
122. dilatory
123. dilettante
124. disconsolate
125. disseminate
126. dissonant
127. distraught
128. dither
129. divest
130. dogged
131. dogmatic
132. dormant
133. droll
134. dub
135. duplicitous
136. eclipse (v.)
137. edify
138. effervescent
139. egregious
140. embark
141. embellish

69. carp
70. censure
71. chary
72. chide
73. churlish
74. circumlocution
75. circumscribed
76. circumvent
77. civility
78. clash
79. coerce
80. cognitive
81. cohere
82. collude
83. comity
84. commiserate
85. commodious
86. compile
87. composure
88. concurrent
89. conscientious
90. consonant (with)
91. conspire
92. constrain
93. construe
94. convoluted
95. copious
96. correlate
97. corroborate
98. cosmopolitan
99. court (v.)
100. covet
101. crafty
102. cramped
103. crass
104. crumble
105. cumbersome
106. cumulative
107. curt

142. eminent
143. empathy
144. epic
145. equanimity
146. equivocate
147. eradicate
148. errant
149. eschew
150. esteem
151. evince
152. exacting
153. exorbitant
154. expunge
155. extant
156. extemporize
157. exuberant
158. fanciful
159. feeble
160. fervid
161. fiat
162. fleet (adj.)
163. flighty
164. flimsy
165. flinch
166. forego
167. forewarn
168. forge (v.)
169. forthright
170. fractious
171. fragile
172. frank
173. fruition
174. furtive
175. fuse
176. gainsay
177. galvanize
178. garish
179. gesticulate
180. giddy

181. glib
182. gloomy
183. glum
184. glut
185. goad
186. grandiloquent
187. grudging
188. grim
189. grueling
190. gruesome
191. hackneyed
192. haughty
193. heckle
194. hedge (v)
195. hoodwink
196. humdrum
197. hyperbole
198. iconoclastic
199. imbroglio
200. immaculate
201. imminent
202. imperative
203. impetuous
204. implacable
205. inane
206. incinerate
207. inclement
208. incongruous
209. indigenous
210. ineluctable
211. inimical
212. inimitable
213. insidious
214. insolvent
215. intertwined
216. intimidate
217. intransigent
218. intrinsic
219. invidious

220. irk
221. jejune
222. judicious
223. justifiable
224. kudos
225. labyrinthine
226. lackluster
227. laudatory
228. lavish
229. limpid
230. listless
231. maladroit
232. malleable
233. mandatory
234. manifest
235. meddlesome
236. meek
237. melancholy
238. mephitic
239. mimic
240. minatory
241. mire (v.)
242. misnomer
243. mitigate
244. mobbed
245. muster
246. nugatory
247. obfuscate
248. obligatory
249. obstinate
250. odious
251. opaque
252. opulent
253. orthodox
254. otiose
255. outmoded
256. overshadow
257. overbearing
258. pang

259. paradigm
260. pariah
261. parsimonious
262. pauper
263. pedantic
264. peerless
265. perceptible
266. perplex
267. peripatetic
268. perspicacious
269. peruse
270. pervasive
271. pester
272. petty
273. philanthropist
274. phlegmatic
275. pine (v.)
276. polemical
277. pragmatic
278. prank
279. precipitate
280. predominate
281. presage
282. prevailing
283. proclivity
284. procrastinate
285. procure
286. prodigy
287. profuse
288. proliferate
289. promulgate
290. pronounced (adj.)
291. propinquity
292. providential
293. provocative
294. prudent
295. pundit
296. pusillanimous
297. quash

298. quell
299. quixotic
300. rambling
301. rank
302. rapt
303. raze
304. rebuff
305. rebuke
306. recalcitrant
307. recluse
308. recurring
309. refrain
310. reiterate
311. relentless
312. reluctant
313. remiss
314. remorse
315. renege
316. renounce
317. repent
318. replete (with)
319. reprieve
320. reprimand
321. reprove
322. repudiate
323. resounding
324. retrieve
325. riddle
326. rife (with)
327. rival
328. roil
329. rookie
330. rudimentary
331. ruminate
332. salient
333. savor
334. scintillating
335. scoff
336. scorn

337. scurrilous
338. servile
339. sift
340. skittish
341. slacken
342. sluggish
343. sly
344. smolder
345. smug
346. snub
347. somber
348. soothe
349. spark (v.)
350. sparse
351. spate
352. splenetic
353. sprawling
354. spur (v.)
355. staunch
356. stealthy
357. stem (v.)
358. stingy
359. stodgy
360. stringent
361. subside
362. subsist
363. succinct
364. sullen
365. supercilious
366. superficial
367. superfluous
368. supersede
369. surfeit
370. susceptible
371. sycophant
372. synoptic
373. taint
374. tantalizing
375. tarnish

376. taunt
377. tedious
378. tendentious
379. tender (v.)
380. tout
381. trifle
382. trivial
383. truncate
384. ulterior
385. underscore
386. unfettered
387. untoward
388. unwonted
389. upbeat
390. usurp
391. vehement
392. verisimilitude
393. viable
394. vicarious
395. vilify
396. virulent
397. vociferous
398. waive
399. wax (v.)
400. wheedle

Supplemental Vocabulary List

Many of the following 500 words have appeared on past GRE exams. Others are likely to appear on exams in the future. Words with a <u>single underline</u> appear in the list "360 Common GRE Words" (pages 75-79) and words with a <u><u>double underline</u></u> appear elsewhere in this Supplemental Vocabulary List. Words in *italics + bold* are related word forms that may also appear on the test.

1. **abase** (v.) humiliate; <u>demean</u>; <u>belittle</u>; besmirch; <u>disparage</u>; <u>denigrate</u>
   abasement (n.)
2. **abashed** (-*ed* adj.) ashamed; embarrassed; humiliated   *abash* (v.)
3. **abet** (v.) aid; assist; support; help
4. **abhor** (v.) dislike; loathe; hate; despise; detest   *abhorrence* (n.)
5. **abject** (adj.) terrible; <u>wretched</u>; <u>dismal</u>; gloomy; hopeless *abjectly* (adv.)
6. **abounding** (adj.) plentiful; abundant; <u>copious</u>; ample; <u>brimming</u>; <u>teeming</u>
7. **abrasive** (adj.) 1) rough; coarse; harsh; rasping 2) rude; insulting; impolite
   abrasively
8. **abridged** (adj.) shortened; abbreviated; curtailed; reduced; truncated
9. **abstemious (adj.)** self-denying; ascetic; self-disciplined; temperate (in one's personal life); moderate
10. **accede** (v.) agree; comply; consent; assent; acquiesce   *accession* (n.)
11. **acclaim** (v.) approve; praise; <u>laud</u>; applaud   *acclaim* (v.)
12. **acquiesce** (v.) comply; agree; submit; give in; accede   *acquiescence* (n.)
13. **adumbrate** (v.) 1) indicate or suggest something about the future; predict; anticipate; foresee; presage; forecast; <u>foreshadow</u> 2) outline; sketch
14. **adverse** (adj.) negative; contrary; opposing   *adversity* (n.)
15. **advocate** (v.) support; speak In favor of; back   *advocate* (agent n.)
16. **affluent** (adj.) wealthy; prosperous; rich; well-to-do   *affluence* (n.)
17. **aftermath** (n.) the result of some action or event; impact; outcome
18. **aggrandize** (v.) exaggerate; overstate; magnify; speak in <u>hyperbole</u>
    aggrandizement (n.)
19. **aghast** (adj.) shocked; horrified; astonished; stunned
20. **agile** (adj.) able to move quickly and gracefully; nimble; graceful   *agility* (n.)
21. **akin (to)** (adj) related; similar; alike
22. **alienate** (v.) become unfriendly with others; become isolated or estranged
    alienation (n.)
23. **allay** (v.) calm; <u>alleviate</u>; relieve; <u>assuage</u>; <u>mitigate</u>; ease
24. **allege** (v.) claim; contend; assert   *alleged* (-*ed* adj.)
    allegation (n.) *allegedly* (adv.)

25. **ameliorate** (v.) improve; make better; enrich; enhance; <u>alleviate</u>
26. **amiss** (adj.) incorrect; mistaken; wrong
27. **anachronistic** (adj.) out of its proper time; outdated; <u>archaic</u> *anachronism* (n.)
28. **analogous** (adj.) similar; comparable; equivalent; corresponding *analogy* (n.)
29. **anecdotal** (adj.) not based on evidence; <u>sketchy</u>; unreliable *anecdotally* (adv.)
30. **antedate** (v.) predate; come before; occur first
31. **apex** (n.) peak; crest; tip; acme; pinnacle; summit; <u>zenith</u>
32. **apocryphal** (adj.) untrue; invented; mythical; fictional
33. **appalling** (adj.) awful; terrible; dreadful; abysmal *appall* (v.)
34. **apparatus** (n.) gadget; device; contraption; mechanism
35. **apposite** (adj.) appropriate; <u>apt</u>; relevant; proper; <u>germane</u>
36. **arable** (adj.) productive; fertile (said of farmland)
37. **arcane** (adj.) mysterious; obscure; <u>recondite</u>; <u>esoteric</u>
38. **articulate** (adj.) <u>eloquent</u>; clear; <u>lucid</u>; expressive
39. **artless** (adj.) innocent; naïve; guileless; ingenuous
40. **aspire** (v.) hope for; desire; have ambitions *aspiration* (n.) *aspirational* (adj.)
41. **assimilate** (v.) integrate; conform; adapt; become part of *assimilation* (n.)
42. **assuage** (v.) appease; relieve; lessen; <u>alleviate</u>; soften; <u>temper</u>; ease; <u>allay</u>; <u>mollify</u>; <u>palliate</u>
43. **attenuate** weaken; lessen; reduce
44. **augment** (v.) supplement; enhance; upgrade; strengthen; boost *augmentation* (n.)
45. **augury** (n.) prediction; forecast; portent; prophecy *augur* (v.)
46. **autochthonous** (adj.) indigenous; aboriginal; original (said of people)
47. **autonomous** (adj.) independent; self-governing; self-sufficient
48. **avaricious** (adj.) greedy; <u>rapacious</u>; acquisitive; avid *avarice* (n.)
49. **aver** (v.) say that something is true; state; claim; affirm
50. **averse (to)** (adj.) against; opposed to; unenthusiastic about *aversion* (n.)
51. **badger** (v.) bother; irritate; <u>pester</u>; harass; <u>irk</u>
52. **balk** (v.) hesitate; <u>recoil</u>; draw back; refuse to go forward; refuse to cooperate
53. **banter** (n.) chat; small talk; witty discussion
54. **begrudge** (v.) resent; be jealous; envy
55. **belittle** (v.) <u>disparage</u>; criticize; <u>demean</u>; <u>abase</u>; <u>berate</u>; <u>defame</u>; <u>besmirch</u>; <u>denigrate</u>
56. **bellicose** (adj.) aggressive; belligerent; warlike; confrontational; hostile; factious *bellicosity* (n.)
57. **bequeath** (v.) donate; bestow; formally give (usually in a will)
58. **berate** (v.) criticize; <u>rebuke</u>; <u>reprimand</u>; scold; demean; <u>belittle</u>; <u>denigrate</u>; <u>disparage</u>; <u>defame</u>; <u>besmirch</u>

59. **beseech** (v.) beg; strongly request; implore; entreat; <u>importune</u>

60. **besmirch** (v.) <u>defame</u>; <u>belittle</u>; <u>demean</u>; <u>abase</u>; <u>berate</u>; <u>denigrate</u>; <u>disparage</u>

61. **bewildered** (adj.) confused; puzzled; dazed; <u>baffled</u>; mystified *bewilder* (v.)
    bewilderment (n.)

62. **blandishment** (n.) flattery; praise; <u>approbation</u>; compliment

63. **blatant** (adj.) obvious; unconcealed; open (said of something negative, such as
    a lie); <u>overt</u> *blatantly* (adv.)

64. **bleak** (adj.) depressing; drab; dreary; <u>austere</u>; desolate; <u>grim</u>

65. **blinkered** (adj.) narrow-minded; having only a limited understanding; inflexible

66. **blissful** (adj.) happy; pleasurable; enjoyable; <u>elated</u> *bliss* (n.)

67. **blunder** (n.) error; mistake; gaffe

68. **bogus** (adj.) false; fake; phony; sham; <u>spurious</u>

69. **boisterous** (adj.) energetic; rowdy; unruly; overexcited

70. **boom** (v.) expand; flourish; prosper; <u>burgeon</u>

71. **boon** (n.) benefit; advantage; help

72. **brimming (with)** (-*ing* adj.) full; overflowing; packed; <u>teeming</u>

73. **brazen** (adj.) <u>blatant</u>; brash; bold; shameless *brazenly* (adv.)

74. **brusque** (adj) <u>curt</u>; abrupt; <u>terse</u>; so quick as to be impolite

75. **bucolic** (adj.) rustic; rural; related to the countryside

76. **budding** (adj.) beginning; <u>nascent</u>; growing; <u>burgeoning</u>; <u>incipient</u>

77. **bulging** (adj.) protruding; distended; swollen

78. **bungle** (v.) mishandle; mismanage; err; botch; make a mistake
    bungling (-*ing* adj.) *bungled* (-*ed* adj)

79. **burdensome** (adj) <u>arduous</u>; <u>onerous</u>; challenging; difficult

80. **cajole** (v.) coax; persuade; <u>entice</u>; <u>wheedle</u>; <u>inveigle</u>; <u>coerce</u>

81. **callous** (adj.) insensitive; heartless; cold *callously* (adv.)

82. **callow** (adj.) immature; rookie; inexperienced; puerile; juvenile

83. **calumny** (n.) lying; slander; slur

84. **cantankerous** (adj;) irritable; <u>irascible</u>; grouchy; grumpy; crabby; <u>peevish</u>;
    testy

85. **capacious** (adj.) roomy; spacious; immense; voluminous; <u>commodious</u>; huge

86. **captious** (n.) critical; <u>acrimonious</u>; <u>petulant</u>

87. **carp** (v.) complain; grumble; <u>quibble</u>; <u>cavil</u>

88. **cavil** (v.) <u>carp</u>; complain; <u>quibble</u>; argue; object

89. **castigate** (v.) criticize; <u>belittle</u>; disgrace; <u>berate</u>; <u>besmirch</u>; <u>defame</u>; <u>disparage</u>;
    <u>denigrate</u>; deprecate

90. **cataclysmic** (adj.) catastrophic; disastrous; ruinous *cataclysm* (n.)

91. **censure** (n.) disapproval; opprobrium; contempt; denunciation
    censorious (adj.)

92. **chary** (adj.) <u>wary</u>; cautious; careful; suspicious

93. **chide** (v.) scold; reprimand; <u>rebuke</u>; nag

94. **churlish** (adj.) rude; <u>boorish</u>; impolite; crude

95. **circumvent** (v.) avoid; evade; <u>elude</u>; get away from *circumvention* (n.)

96. **civility** (n.) politeness; courtesy; respect

97. **clash** (v.) quarrel; <u>squabble</u>; argue; spar

98. **cloying** (-ing adj.) 1) sickening; sickly-sweet; sugary 2) overly sentimental

99. **coerce** (v.) force; persuade; pressure; compel; twist someone's arm
   coercive (adj)

100. **cognitive** (adj.) mental; related to thinking *cognition* (n.)

101. **cohere** (v.) adhere; bind; stick to *coherence* (n.) *cohesive* (adj.)

102. **collude (with)** (v.) conspire; plot; plan to do something negative *collusion* (n.)

103. **commend** (v.) praise; laud; extol; acclaim *commendation* (n.)
   commendable (adj.)

104. **comity** (n.) harmony; concord; friendliness; <u>cordiality</u>

105. **commodious** (adj.) spacious; roomy; <u>capacious</u>; huge; immense

106. **compelling** (adj.) convincing; persuasive; believable

107. **compile** (v.) collect; gather; bring together; accumulate; amass
   compilation (n.)

108. **composure** (n.) equanimity; calmness; serenity; poise; tranquility
   composed (-ed adj.)

109. **compunction** (n.) regret; hesitation; <u>qualm</u>

110. **concomitant** (adj.) associated with; related; simultaneous; concurrent

111. **congruent** (adj.) harmonious; matching; consistent; similar *congruence* (n.)

112. **conscientious** careful; thorough; reliable; <u>sedulous</u>; <u>meticulous</u>; <u>scrupulous</u>

113. **conspire** (v.) plot; collude; plan to do something (usually something negative)
   conspiracy (n.) *conspirator* (agent n.)

114. **constrain** (v.) coerce; force; compel; pressure *constraint* (n.)

115. **construe** (v.) understand as; interpret; define as *misconstrue* (neg. v.)

116. **convoluted** (adj.) intricate; <u>tortuous</u>; involved; complicated; complex

117. **corroborate** (v.) support; confirm; verify; validate; substantiate; <u>buttress</u>

118. **cosmopolitan** (n.) international; worldly; sophisticated

119. **court** (v.) <u>woo</u>; attract; <u>allure</u>

120. **covet** (v.) crave; desire; want *covetous* (adj.)

121. **cower** (v.) cringe; recoil; retreat in fear *cowering* (-ing adj.)

122. **crafty** (adj.) <u>sly</u>; sneaky; cunning; <u>wily</u>; <u>sly</u>; <u>canny</u>; <u>shrewd</u>

123. **cramped** (adj.) small and uncomfortable; overcrowded; confining

124. **crass** (adj.) insensitive; rude; <u>boorish</u>; <u>churlish</u>; impolite; crude

125. **crumble** (v.) fall apart; disintegrate; break into pieces

126. **cull** (v.) pick out; select; <u>winnow</u>; glean

127. **cumbersome** (adj.) awkward; bulky; <u>burdensome</u>

128. **curt** (adj.) <u>brusque</u>; abrupt; so quick as to be rude

129. **dank** (adj.) damp, chilly; moist; clammy

130. **debased** (*-ed* adj.) corrupt; degraded; <u>besmirched</u>; *debase* (v.)

131. **debilitating** (adj) devastating; <u>enervating</u>; weakening

132. **debunk** (v.) expose the truth; demystify

133. **decry** (v.) complain; carp; gripe; grumble; <u>quibble</u>

134. **deface** (v.) ruin; <u>mar</u>; spoil; disfigure

135. **deft** (adj.) skillful; competent; capable; adroit

136. **defame** (v.) criticize; <u>disparage</u>; <u>deprecate</u>; <u>demean</u>; <u>belittle</u>; <u>besmirch</u>; <u>berate</u>

137. **defraud** (v.) cheat; deceive; swindle; trick

138. **degrade** (v.) damage; destroy; reduce *degrading* (*-ing* adj.)

139. **demean** (v.) criticize; <u>belittle</u>; disgrace; <u>berate</u>; <u>castigate</u>; <u>besmirch</u>; <u>defame</u>; <u>disparage</u>; <u>denigrate</u>; deprecate *demeaning* (-ing adj.)

140. **demur** (v.) object; doubt; protest; <u>balk</u>

141. **demure** (adj) modest; decorous; shy; <u>diffident</u> *demurely* (adv.)

142. **deride** (v.) ridicule; <u>scorn</u>; mock; disdain; <u>disparage</u>; <u>denigrate</u>; <u>defame</u>; <u>scoff</u> *derision* (n.)

143. **derogatory** (adj.) <u>disparaging</u>; critical; insulting; offensive; <u>pejorative</u>

144. **descry** (v.) spot; see; observe; notice; perceive; <u>espy</u>

145. **despondent** (adj.) unhappy; <u>morose</u>; depressed; downhearted; dejected

146. **deter** (v.) discourage; daunt; prevent *deterrent* (n.)

147. **deteriorate** (v.) worsen; decline; weaken; <u>wane</u>; get worse **deterioration** (n.)

148. **devoid (of)** (adj.) empty; barren; lacking

149. **didactic** (adj.) educational; informative; instructive

150. **dilapidated** (adj.) run-down; in poor condition; <u>ramshackle</u>; decrepit

151. **dilatory** (adj.) slow; delaying; tardy

152. **din** (n.) noise; <u>cacophony</u>; commotion; hubbub

153. **dirge** (n.) a funeral song; a slow, sad song

154. **discomfit** (v.) embarrass; disconcert; distress; fluster *discomfited* (*-ed* adj.)

155. **disconsolate** (adj.) unhappy; <u>gloomy</u>; <u>somber</u>; <u>morose</u>; forlorn

156. **disparity** (n.) difference; discrepancy; lack of equality

157. **disquiet** (n.) anxiety; worry; alarm; uneasiness

158. **dissonant** (adj.) discordant; inharmonious; <u>cacophonous</u>

159. **distended** (adj.) <u>bulging</u>; protruding; sticking out *distend* (v.)

160. **distraught** (adj.) distressed; upset; worried; anxious

161. **dither** (v.) fail to make a decision; hesitate; <u>waver</u>; dally; <u>vacillate</u>

162. **divest** (v.) get rid of; separate from; lose

163. **docile** (adj.) passive; <u>compliant</u>; submissive; <u>meek</u>; obedient

164. **dogged** (adj.) stubborn; resolute; firm; <u>obstinate</u>; <u>intractable</u>, <u>pertinacious</u>; intransigent; adamant *doggedly* (adv.)

165. **dogmatic** (adj) rigid; inflexible; unbending; uncompromising *dogmatically* (adv.)

166. **dormant** (adj.) sleeping; inactive; <u>latent</u>; hidden *dormancy* (n.)

167. **dour** (adj.) <u>bleak</u>; <u>glum</u>; <u>gloomy</u>; <u>morose</u>; surly

168. **draconian** (adj.) strict; harsh; severe; oppressive (said of laws)

169. **droll** (adj.) funny; humorous; comic; witty; amusing

170. **dub** (v.) name; call; designate; nickname

171. **dupe** (v.) cheat; <u>defraud</u>; <u>hoodwink</u>; swindle

172. **duplicitous** (adj.) tricky; cheating; conniving; dishonest; deceitful *duplicity* (n.)

173. **eclipse** (v.) hide; conceal; obscure

174. **edify** (v.) enlighten; inform; instruct; teach

175. **effervescent** (adj.) sparkling; bubbly; lively; <u>spirited</u>

176. **efficacious** (adj.) efficient; effective; successful

177. **egregious** (adj.) terrible; awful; shocking; <u>deplorable</u>

178. **elated** (adj.) excited; overjoyed; ecstatic; euphoric; jubilant *elate* (v.) *elation* (n.)

179. **eloquent** (adj.) articulate; well-spoken; expressive; persuasive *eloquence* (n.) *eloquently* (adv.)

180. **emancipate** (v.) liberate; free; release *emancipation* (n.) *emancipated* (-ed adj.)

181. **embark** (v.) leave; board (a plane, ship, etc.); depart *embarkation* (n.)

182. **embellish** (v.) enhance; add to; exaggerate; embroider *embellishment* (n.)

183. **emend** (v.) revise; edit; amend; alter; correct *emendation* (n.)

184. **eminent** (adj.) famous; well-known; celebrated; renowned; distinguished *eminence* (n.) *eminently* (adv.)

185. **empathy** (n.) understanding; sympathy; compassion *empathize* (v.) *empathetic* (adj.)

186. **engaging** (adj.) attractive; appealing; <u>alluring</u>; pleasing

187. **ennui** (n.) weariness; boredom; <u>languor</u>

188. **epic** (adj.) grand; classic; larger-than-life; impressive

189. **equanimity** (n.) calmness; <u>composure</u>; self-control; poise

190. **equivocate** (v.) <u>quibble</u>; <u>dissemble</u>; <u>prevaricate</u>; evade the truth

191. **eradicate** (v.) destroy; remove; eliminate; get rid of; <u>vitiate</u>

192. **errant** (adj.) badly behaved; naughty; misbehaving; wayward

193. **eschew** (v.) avoid; shun; <u>abstain</u>

194. **espy** (v.) spot; notice; observe; discern; <u>descry</u>

195. **esteem** (v.) admire; respect; approve; look up to *esteem* (n.)

196. **estranged** (*-ed* adj.) alienated; separated from; disaffected
197. **euphoric** (adj.) happy; <u>jubilant</u>; <u>elated</u>; excited; joyful; ecstatic *euphoria* (n.)
198. **evanescent** (adj.) <u>fleeting</u>; temporary; <u>transitory</u>
199. **evince** (v.) show; demonstrate; display; reveal; exhibit; disclose
200. **exacting** (adj.) demanding; rigorous; thorough; requiring precision; challenging
201. **excoriate** (v.) criticize; <u>berate</u>; <u>belittle</u>; <u>castigate</u>; <u>demean</u>; <u>upbraid</u>; <u>rebuke</u>
202. **exemplary** (adj.) standard; model; typical; archetype
203. **exhort** (v.) urge; encourage; insist *exhortation* (n.)
204. **exonerate** (v.) exculpate; free from guilt; prove innocent
205. **exorbitant** (adj.) unreasonable (said of prices); overpriced; expensive
206. **expostulate** (v.) argue; disagree; object; remonstrate; complain
207. **expunge** (v.) delete; erase; obliterate; remove
208. **extant** (adj.) existent; present; surviving
209. **extirpate** (v.) delete; eliminate; expunge; remove; purge; obliterate; <u>vitiate</u>
210. **extrapolate** (v.) guess about the future based on present information *extrapolation* (n.)
211. **extricate** (v.) remove; pull out; extract; detach; free
212. **exuberant** (adj.) high-spirited; enthusiastic; <u>ebullient</u>; <u>elated</u>; <u>jubilant</u> **exuberance** (n.)
213. **fanciful** (adj.) imaginary; fantastic; unbelievable
214. **fawning** (adj.) <u>obsequious</u>; submissive; flattering; <u>servile</u>
215. **feeble** (adj.) weak; frail; delicate *feebly* (adv.)
216. **ferocious** (adj.) fierce; vicious; aggressive; savage
217. **fervid** (adj.) enthusiastic; <u>zealous</u>; <u>ardent</u>; <u>fervent</u>
218. **fiasco** (n.) disaster; failure; debacle
219. **fickle** (adj.) indecisive; <u>capricious</u>; <u>irresolute</u>; unpredictable; whimsical; <u>flighty</u>
220. **fleet** (adj.) fast; quick; rapid
221. **flighty** (adj.) changeable; erratic; unreliable; capricious; <u>fickle</u>
222. **flimsy** (adj.) weak; <u>fragile</u>; easily breakable
223. **flippant** (adj.) <u>facetious</u>; frivolous; silly
224. **flinch** (v.) <u>recoil</u>; <u>balk</u>; <u>cringe</u>; show fear
225. **florid** (adj.) ornate; elaborate; <u>flamboyant</u>; garish; showy; <u>gaudy</u>
226. **foe** (n.) enemy; opponent; <u>rival</u>; adversary
227. **foment** (v.) <u>stimulate</u>; provoke; incite
228. **foreboding** (adj.) <u>ominous</u>; threatening; menacing; <u>sinister</u>
229. **foreshadow** (v.) indicate something about the future; adumbrate; predict; presage

230. **forge** (v.) 1) create; make; produce 2) copy; counterfeit; falsify
231. **forthright** (adj.) honest; open; frank; candid
232. **fortuitous** (adj.) 1) accidental; unintended 2) lucky; fortunate
    fortuitously (adv.)
233. **fractious** (adj.) irritable; irascible; truculent; peevish; petulant; testy
234. **fragile** (adj.) breakable; flimsy; brittle *fragility* (n.)
235. **fragmentary** (adj.) incomplete; disconnected; patchy; broken
236. **frank** (adj.) candid; forthright; open; honest; guileless
237. **fruition** (n.) completion; realization; execution; fulfillment
238. **fulminate** (v.) speak critically or angrily; rage; rant; castigate; inveigh against
239. **furtive** (adj) secretive; sly; sneaky; clandestine; covert *furtively* (adv.)
240. **fuse** (v.) join; unite; connect *fusion* (n.)
241. **gainsay** (v.) deny; refute; contradict
242. **galvanize** (v.) energize; electrify; stimulate
243. **gamut** (n.) range; scale; spectrum
244. **garish** (adj.) gaudy; showy; flashy
245. **gesticulate** (v.) gesture; signal
246. **giddy** (adj.) dizzy; light-headed; unsteady *giddiness* (n.)
247. **gloomy** (adj.) melancholy; morose; somber; depressed; forlorn; glum
248. **glum** (adj.) gloomy; morose; sad; somber, depressed; forlorn
249. **glut** (n.) excess; superfluity; surfeit; surplus; plethora
250. **goad** (v.) stimulate; prod; motivate; get moving
251. **grandiloquent** (adj.) speaking in an elevated style; bombastic; pompous;
    high-sounding
252. **grim** (adj.) unattractive; desolate; forbidding; drab; dreary; dismal; bleak
253. **grudging** (adj.) reluctant; unwilling; complaining *grudgingly* (adv.)
254. **grueling** (adj.) difficult; challenging; onerous; arduous; exhausting
255. **gruesome** (adj.) horrible; awful; shocking; ghastly
256. **hackneyed** (adj.) trite; banal; stale; commonplace
257. **halcyon** (adj.) peaceful; tranquil; calm
258. **harp (on)** (v.) nag; bother; harass; pester; keep talking about
259. **harrowing** (adj.) frightening; traumatic; terrifying; worrying
260. **haughty** (v.) arrogant; self-important; conceited; overbearing
261. **hectic** (adj.) extremely busy; frantic; frenetic; frenzied
262. **hedge** (v.) prevaricate; dissemble; equivocate; evade the truth
263. **hoodwink** (v.) deceive; trick; defraud; dupe
264. **humdrum** (adj.) dull; boring; banal; everyday; quotidian
265. **hyperbole** (n.) a deliberate exaggeration; overstatement; embellishment
    hyperbolic (adj.)

266. **iconoclastic** (adj.) non-traditional; revolutionary; radical *iconoclast* (agent n.)

267. **imbroglio** (n.) confusion; fiasco; complication; entanglement

268. **immaculate** (adj.) spotless; clean; perfect; tidy *immaculately* (adv.)

269. **imminent** (adj.) impending; looming; forthcoming; about to happen

270. **immutable** (adj.) invariable; unchangeable; absolute; undeniable; indisputable

271. **impetuous** (adj.) rash; hasty; impulsive; sudden; unthinking; capricious *impetuously* (adv.)

272. **implacable** (adj.) ruthless; cruel; cold-hearted; merciless **implacably** (adv.)

273. **impugn** (v.) question; doubt; dispute; challenge

274. **inane** (adj.) silly; frivolous; childish; flippant

275. **incinerate** (v.) burn up completely; set fire to

276. **incipient** (v.) emerging; developing; inchoate; initial; budding

277. **incongruous** (adj.) inconsistent; odd; incompatible; out of the ordinary *incongruity* (n.)

278. **inculcate** (v.) teach; instruct; indoctrinate; instill; inform

279. **indigenous** (adj.) native; autochthonous; original (said of people)

280. **ineluctable** (adj.) unstoppable; inevitable; inexorable; unavoidable

281. **inexorable** (adj.) unstoppable; inevitable; ineluctable; unavoidable

282. **infringe (on)** (v.) interfere with; trespass; encroach on *infringement* (n.)

283. **inimical** (adj.) hostile; unfriendly; antagonistic

284. **inimitable** (adj.) unique; matchless; incomparable

285. **inkling** (n.) suggestion; hint; hunch; notion; idea

286. **insidious** (adj.) sneaky; crafty; pernicious; treacherous; sinister

287. **insolvent** (adj.) bankrupt; broke; impecunious; destitute; penurious *insolvency* (n.)

288. **insouciant** (adj.) easy-going; carefree; nonchalant; untroubled; lighthearted

289. **intertwined** (adj.) entangled; knotted; interwoven; tied together

290. **intimidate** (v.) frighten; daunt; scare; threaten; terrorize

291. **intractable** (adj.) stubborn; obstinate; obdurate; uncompromising; inflexible; pertinacious; intransigent

292. **intransigent** (adj.) stubborn; intractable; obstinate; obdurate; uncompromising; inflexible; pertinacious

293. **intrinsic** (adj.) innate; inborn, inherent; central; basic *intrinsically* (adv.)

294. **inveigh (against)** (v.) protest; complain; fulminate; rail against

295. **inveigle** (v.) entice; cajole; persuade; wheedle; coax

296. **invidious** (adj.) unpleasant; undesirable; loathsome; hateful; odious

297. **irk** (v.) anger; vex; bother; irritate; rankle

298. **iterate** (v.) say again; repeat; emphasize; reiterate *iteration* (n.)

299. **jejune** (adj.) boring; <u>inane</u>; <u>insipid</u>; <u>banal</u>; <u>bland</u>

300. **jubilant** (adj.) excited; happy; <u>euphoric</u>; <u>elated</u>; triumphant *jubilation* (n.)

301. **judicious** (adj.) sensible; cautious; careful; <u>astute</u>; <u>shrewd</u>; <u>canny</u>; clever *judiciously* (adv.)

302. **justifiable** (adj.) reasonable; correct; proper; acceptable; legitimate *justify* (v.) *unjustifiable* (neg. adj.)

303. **kindle** (v.) spark; ignite; light on fire; start some action

304. **kudos** (n.) praise; <u>acclaim</u>; <u>approbation</u>; commendation; congratulations

305. **labyrinthine** (adj.) complex; involved; <u>tortuous</u>; <u>convoluted</u>; tangled *labyrinth* (n.)

306. **lackluster** (adj.) boring; <u>bland</u>; <u>insipid</u>; undistinguished

307. **languorous** (adj.) lazy; languid; <u>indolent</u>; <u>lethargic</u>; <u>sluggish</u>; slothful; <u>listless</u> *languor* (n/)

308. **latent** (adj.) hidden; <u>covert</u>; <u>dormant</u>; suppressed; inactive *latency* (n.)

309. **laud** (v.) praise; <u>acclaim</u>; applaud; commend; congratulate *laudatory* (adj.)

310. **lavish** (adj.) luxurious; rich; <u>plush</u>; <u>sumptuous</u>; extravagant; lush   (v.) give; be generous *lavishly* (adv.)

311. **lexicon** (n.) vocabulary; list of words; jargon; lexis

312. **limpid** (adj.) clear; transparent; sheer; crystalline; <u>pellucid</u>

313. **listless** lazy; inactive; <u>indolent</u>; <u>enervated</u>; <u>lethargic</u>; <u>sluggish</u>

314. **loom** (v.) 1) appear; emerge; materialize 2) hang over; seem large

315. **magnanimous** (adj.) generous; charitable; unstinting; benevolent *magnanimously* (adv.)

316. **maladroit** (adj.) <u>inept</u>; incompetent; <u>feckless</u>; clumsy

317. **malleable** (adj.) able to be molded; pliable; plastic; flexible *malleability* (n.)

318. **mandatory** (adj.) necessary; required; compulsory; <u>obligatory</u>

319. **manifest** (adj.) obvious; apparent; evident; patent; <u>pronounced</u>; <u>overt</u>; <u>blatant</u> *manifestation* (n.) *manifestly* (adv.)

320. **marginal** (adj.) unimportant; peripheral; insignificant; on the fringe

321. **maudlin** (adj.) overly sentimental; overemotional; syrupy; <u>mawkish</u>

322. **mawkish** (adj.) <u>maudlin</u>; mushy; overly sentimental

323. **meddlesome** (adj.) interfering; intrusive; <u>officious</u>; nosey *meddle* (v.) *meddling* (n.)

324. **meditative** (adj.) thoughtful; <u>pensive</u>; contemplative; reflective

325. **meek** (adj.) humble; timid; docile; compliant; complaisant *meekly* (adv.)

326. **melancholic** (adj.) sad; <u>gloomy</u>; <u>glum</u>; <u>morose</u>; <u>somber</u>; forlorn *melancholy* (n.)

327. **mephitic** (adj.) smelly; foul-smelling; <u>malodorous</u>; stinky

328. **mimic** (v.) copy; imitate; <u>emulate</u>; ape *mimicry* (n.) *mimic* (agent n.)

329. **minatory** (adj.) warning; alarming; dangerous; dire; <u>portentous</u>; <u>ominous</u>; threatening

330. **mishap** (n.) misfortune; accident; an unfortunate event

331. **mitigate** (v.) lessen; ease; improve; moderate; <u>assuage</u>; <u>alleviate</u>
mitigating (-ing adj.)

332. **mobbed** (adj.) crowded; surrounded; swarming; <u>teeming with</u>; clogged

333. **mogul** (n.) powerful businessperson; tycoon; wealthy person; magnate

334. **mull** (v.) consider; think about; ponder; contemplate; muse; <u>ruminate</u>

335. **nascent** (adj.) emerging; developing; <u>inchoate</u>; <u>burgeoning</u>; <u>budding</u>; <u>incipient</u>

336. **nebulous** (adj.) unclear; vague; imprecise; hazy

337. **nefarious** (adj.) evil; wicked; despicable; loathsome; vile; <u>odious</u>

338. **nonplussed** (adj.) confused; <u>baffled</u>; <u>bewildered</u>; puzzled; mystified

339. **nuance** (n.) subtle difference; slight distinction *nuanced* (-ed adj.)

340. **nugatory** (adj.) trivial; <u>petty</u>; unimportant; trifling; irrelevant

341. **obeisance** (n.) submissiveness; obedience; respect; <u>deference</u>; <u>obsequiousness</u>; *obeisant* (adj.)

342. **obfuscate** (v.) confuse; complicate; mystify; muddle; obscure *obfuscation* (n,)

343. **obligatory** (adj.) required; <u>mandatory</u>; compulsory; necessary *obligation* (n.)

344. **obsequious** (adj.) submissive; respectful; deferential; obeisant
obsequiousness (n.) *obsequiously* (adv.)

345. **obstinate** (adj.) stubborn; <u>dogged</u>; uncompromising; resolute; <u>intransigent</u>; <u>intractable</u>; <u>obdurate</u>; <u>pertinacious</u>; adamant

346. **odious** (adj.) hateful; abhorrent; loathsome; repellent; <u>invidious</u>

347. **ominous** (adj.) threatening; warning; worrying; menacing; <u>sinister</u> *omen* (n.)
ominously (adv.)

348. **opaque** (adj.) difficult to see through; clouded; blurred; murky; impenetrable; difficult to understand *opacity* (n.)

349. **opprobrium** (n.) criticism; <u>scorn</u>; contempt; <u>censure</u>; disapproval; ridicule

350. **opulent** (adj.) luxurious; wealthy; <u>plush</u>; lavish; <u>sumptuous</u>; affluent
opulence (n.)

351. **orthodox** (adj.) conventional; standard; traditional; established *orthodoxy* (n.)

352. **otiose** (adj.) futile; pointless; ineffective; useless

353. **outmoded** (adj.) old fashioned; out of date; antiquated; obsolete

354. **overshadow** (v.) dominate; surpass; outdo; <u>eclipse</u>

355. **overbearing** (adj.) domineering; <u>imperious</u>; bossy; authoritative;

356. **overweening** (adj.) arrogant; <u>haughty</u>; conceited

357. **palatable** (adj.) acceptable; agreeable; pleasant; attractive; tempting

358. **palliate** (v.) <u>alleviate</u>; <u>assuage</u>; <u>abate</u>; allay; <u>mitigate</u>; <u>temper</u>; diminish; relieve *palliative* (adj.) *palliative* (n.)

359. **pan** (v.) criticize; <u>berate</u>; critique

360. **pang** (n.) pain; twinge; spasm

361. **paradigm** (n.) model; pattern; standard; <u>paragon</u>; <u>template</u>

362. **paragon** (n.) a perfect example; model; archetype; ideal; <u>paradigm</u>

363. **pariah** (agent n.) outcast; exile; outsider

364. **parsimonious** (adj.) <u>frugal</u>; <u>thrifty</u>; <u>miserly</u>; <u>stingy</u>

365. **pauper** (agent n.) a very poor person; an <u>indigent</u> person

366. **pedantic** (adj.) <u>pompous</u>; <u>abstruse</u>; <u>didactic</u>

367. **pellucid** (adj.) clear; transparent; limpid; crystalline

368. **peerless** (adj.) incomparable; unequaled; matchless; unique

369. **peevish** (adj.) <u>irascible</u>; irritable; easily annoyed; grumpy; testy; cranky; crabby

370. **pejorative** (adj.) <u>derogatory</u>; negative; offensive; uncomplimentary; insulting

371. **penchant** (n.) desire; <u>proclivity</u>; affinity; predilection

372. **perceptible** (adj.) <u>tangible</u>; observable; noticeable; <u>palpable</u> *perceive* (v.) *perception* (n.) *perceptibly* (adv.) *imperceptible* (neg. adj.)

373. **perennial** (adj.) happening again and again; <u>recurring</u>; continuing; persistent

374. **perfidious** (adj.) <u>treacherous</u>; disloyal; dishonest; deceitful *perfidy* (n.)

375. **pernicious** (adj.) evil; malicious; wicked; spiteful; <u>nefarious</u> *perniciously* (adv.)

376. **perspicuous** (adj.) seeing things clearly; <u>astute</u> *perspicuity* (n.)

377. **perplex** (v.) <u>baffle</u>; mystify; puzzle; stump *perplexing* (-*ing* adj.) *perplexed* (-*ed* adj.)

378. **peripatetic** (adj.) <u>itinerant</u>; nomadic; travelling; wayfaring; roaming

379. **perspicacious** (adj.) <u>astute</u>; intelligent; <u>erudite</u>; wise; <u>sage</u>

380. **pertinacious** (adj.) stubborn; <u>obstinate</u>; resolute; <u>intransigent</u>; headstrong; intractable

381. **pertinent** (adj.) relevant; <u>germane</u>; <u>apposite</u>; related *pertinence* (n.)

382. **peruse** (v.) scan; look over; examine; <u>scrutinize</u> *perusal* (n.)

383. **pervasive** (adj.) <u>ubiquitous</u>; universal; permeating; <u>rife</u>

384. **pester** (v.) annoy; harass; disturb; irritate; nag; <u>vex</u> *pest* (agent n.)

385. **petty** (adj.) trivial; unimportant; minor; insignificant; <u>nugatory</u> *pettiness* (n.)

386. **philanthropist** (agent n.) contributor; sponsor; humanitarian; donor *philanthropy* (n.)

387. **phlegmatic** (adj.) calm; unemotional; unconcerned; detached; <u>impassive</u>; <u>apathetic</u>; <u>indifferent</u>

388. **pine** (v.) desire; long for; yearn; crave; want

389. **pinpoint** (v.) locate exactly; identify

390. **ploy** (n.) trick; plan; tactic; ruse; scheme; stratagem

391. **polemical** (adj.) belligerent; combative; argumentative; bellicose; pugnacious; contentious

392. **pompous** (adj.) self-important; arrogant; haughty; pretentious *pomposity* (n.)

393. **portentous** (adj.) 1) ominous; alarming; threatening; looming 2) important; significant; crucial *portent* (n.)

394. **postulate** (v.) assume; theorize; hypothesize; suppose *postulation* (n.)

395. **potable** (adj.) drinkable; clean (said of water); fit to drink

396. **pragmatic** (adj.) practical; realistic; sensible; hard-headed; reasonable *pragmatism* (n.) *pragmatist* (agent n.) *pragmatically* (adv.)

397. **prank** (n.) trick; joke; hoax *prankster* (agent n.)

398. **preamble** (n.) introduction; opening; prelude

399. **precipitate** (adj.) hasty; swift; rushed; impulsive; crash

400. **predominant** (adj.) dominant; leading; most important; controlling; prevailing *predominate* (v.) *predominately* (adv.)

401. **prevailing** (adj.) leading; dominant; main; most important; prevalent; predominant

402. **proclivity** (adj.) tendency; penchant; inclination; predilection

403. **procrastinate** (v.) postpone; delay; defer

404. **procure** (v.) obtain; acquire; secure *procurement* (n.)

405. **prodigal** (adj.) wasteful; reckless with money or resources; profligate

406. **prodigy** (agent n.) young genius; wonder; sensation

407. **profuse** (adj.) plentiful; copious; bountiful; abundant; teeming; abounding; ample *profusion* (n.)

408. **proliferate** (v.) increase; thrive; burgeon; multiply *proliferation* (n.)

409. **promulgate** (v.) spread; disseminate; publicize; propagate; broadcast

410. **pronounced** (adj.) noticeable; obvious; evident; distinct; manifest

411. **propinquity** (n.) nearness; proximity; close relationship

412. **propriety** (n.) politeness; decorum; appropriateness; good manners

413. **provincial** (adj.) narrow-minded; insular; unsophisticated

414. **provocative** (adj.) challenging; provoking; stimulating; inflammatory *provoke* (v.) *provocation* (n.)

415. **prudent** (adj.) sensible; careful; judicious; cautious *prudence* (n.) *prudently* (adv.)

416. **pry** (v.) interfere; inquire into; meddle; poke into

417. **punctilious** (adj.) scrupulous; assiduous; meticulous; conscientious; thorough; sedulous; diligent

418. **pundit** (agent n.) expert; commentator; analyst; authority *punditry* (n.)

419. **pusillanimous** (adj.) cowardly; craven; timid; fearful; timorous; apprehensive

420. **quash** (v.) suppress; crush; repress; defeat; subdue; quell

421. **quell** (v.) suppress; subdue; quash; control; defeat

422. **quench** (v.) slake; sate; satisfy (said of thirst)

423. **quixotic** (adj.) idealistic; impractical; romantic; unrealistic; dreamy

424. **rambling** (adj.) confused; incoherent; wordy; verbose; prolix; garrulous

425. **ramshackle** (adj.) run-down; dilapidated; decrepit; in poor repair; crumbling

426. **rancorous** (adj.) acrimonious; bitter; malicious; acerbic; mordant; scathing; trenchant *rancor* (n.)

427. **rankle** (v.) irritate; annoy; irk; gall; vex; bother

428. **rapt** (adj.) fascinated; engrossed; focused; enthralled

429. **raze** (v.) destroy; topple; demolish; annihilate

430. **rebuff** (v.) reject; refuse; turn away; rebuke *rebuff* (n.)

431. **rebuke** (v.) disapprove; admonish; condemn; rebuff *rebuke* (n.)

432. **recalcitrant** (adj.) stubborn; intractable; obstinate; inflexible; dogged; obdurate; intransigent

433. **recluse** (agent n.) hermit; loner; outsider

434. **recurring** (adj.) repeating; happening again and again; perennial; rhythmic; habitual *recurrence* (n.)

435. **refrain (from)** (v.) avoid; abstain; renounce; forego; quit; give up

436. **reiterate** (v.) repeat; retell; restate; echo; iterate

437. **relentless** (adj.) persistent; inexorable; ceaseless *relentlessly* (adv.)

438. **reluctant** (adj.) unwilling; disinclined; unenthusiastic *reluctance* (n.) *reluctantly* (adv.)

439. **remonstrate** (v.) argue; object; complain; squabble; bicker; quarrel

440. **remorse** (n.) regret; sorrow; guilt *remorseful* (adj.)

441. **renounce** (v.) reject; refuse; spurn; leave behind; abandon

442. **replete (with)** (adj.) full; complete; abounding; rife; teeming

443. **repress** (v.) suppress; hold down; curb; limit; stifle *repression* (n.) *repressive* (adj.)

444. **reprimand** (v.) scold; warn; reprove; rebuke

445. **reprove** (v.) criticize; scold; reprimand; rebuke

446. **repudiate** (v.) reject; not accept; deny; rebut *repudiation* (n.)

447. **retrieve** (v.) get back; recover; regain *retrieval* (n.)

448. **riddle** (n.) puzzle; enigma; conundrum; mystery

449. **risible** (adj.) humorous; funny; laughable; cheerful; droll *risibly* (adv.)

450. **rival** (v.) vie; compete; contend *rival* (v.) *rival* (agent n.) *rivalry* (n.)

451. **robust** (adj.) healthy; vigorous; strong; powerful

452. **roil** (v.) 1) mix; stir; blend 2) anger; annoy; <u>vex</u>

453. **rookie** (n.) beginner; <u>novice</u>; <u>tyro</u>; <u>neophyte</u>; <u>fledgling</u>

454. **rudimentary** (adj.) basic; elementary; fundamental *rudiment* (n.)

455. **rueful** (adj.) regretful; <u>remorseful</u>; contrite; apologetic *rue* (v.)
ruefully (adv.)

456. **ruminate** (v.) think over; ponder; reflect; contemplate; <u>mull</u>

457. **salient** (adj.) <u>pronounced</u>; noticeable; striking; dramatic; prominent; significant

458. **savor** (v.) taste; enjoy *savory* (adj.)

459. **scintillating** (adj.) 1) sparkling; brilliant; dazzling; glittering; shining
2) amusing; fascinating

460. **scoff** (v.) ridicule; jeer; laugh at; mock; <u>deride</u>

461. **scorn** (n.) contempt; disdain; disrespect; <u>derision</u>; ridicule *scornful* (adj.)

462. **scrupulous** (adj.) 1) <u>assiduous</u>; <u>meticulous</u>; <u>conscientious</u>; <u>sedulous</u>;
painstaking; <u>diligent</u>, <u>punctilious</u> 2) honorable; moral; trusty *scrupulously* (adv.)

463. **scurrilous** (adj.) slanderous; insulting; verbally abusive; offensive

464. **servile** (adj.) obedient; submissive; <u>fawning</u>; subservient; <u>obsequious</u>;
<u>obeisant</u> *servility* (n.)

465. **sinister** (adj.) menacing; <u>ominous</u>; threatening; dangerous

466. **skittish** (adj.) <u>wary</u>; uneasy; nervous; anxious; edgy

467. **slake** (v.) <u>quench</u>; sate; satisfy (said of thirst)

468. **slipshod** (adj.) careless; sloppy; casual

469. **sluggish** (adj.) slow-moving; <u>lethargic</u>; <u>listless</u>; <u>indolent</u>; slothful; <u>enervated</u>;
languorous; <u>torpid</u> *sluggishness* (n.)

470. **sly** (adj.) <u>canny</u>; <u>crafty</u>; cunning; clever; <u>shrewd</u>; tricky *slyly* (adv.)

471. **smug** (adj.) self-satisfied; arrogant; conceited; haughty; snobbish *smugness*
(n.) *smugly* (adv.)

472. **snub** (v.) reject; impolitely ignore; insult; humiliate *snub* (n.)

473. **solemn** (adj.) <u>somber</u>; formal; dignified; reflective; sober; staid **solemnity** (n.)
solemnize (v.) **solemnly** (adv.)

474. **soothe** (v.) calm; <u>pacify</u>; <u>mollify</u>; <u>appease</u>; <u>assuage</u>; <u>placate</u> *soothing* (-ing adj.)

475. **spark** (n.) <u>stimulus</u>; catalyst; spur; trigger *spark* (v.)

476. **sparse** (adj.) scant; light; scarce; <u>meager</u> *sparsely* (adv.)

477. **spirited** (adj.) lively; energetic; vigorous

478. **splenetic** (adj.) ill-tempered; peevish; <u>irascible</u>; <u>fractious</u>; grumpy;
<u>cantankerous</u>; crabby

479. **spur** (v.) <u>stimulate</u>; <u>spark</u>; <u>goad</u>; provoke; encourage

480. **staid** (adj.) quiet; calm; <u>quiescent</u>; <u>solemn</u>; formal

481. **stately** (adj.) formal; grand; dignified; majestic

482. **staunch** (adj.) loyal; dependable; reliable; faithful; steadfast (v.) slow; curb; stem; hinder; restrict

483. **stealthy** (adj.) secretive; sneaky; surreptitious; sly; furtive; crafty; wily **stealth** (n.) **stealthily** (adv.)

484. **stem** (v.) stop; slow down; curtail; curb; hinder; hamper

485. **stifle** (v.) 1) suppress; repress; hold down **stifling** (-ing adj.)
    2) **stem from** (v.) come from; grow from

486. **stingy** (adj.) miserly; parsimonious; cheap; penny-pinching **stinginess** (n.)

487. **stolid** (adj.) impassive; unemotional; phlegmatic; detached; unconcerned; apathetic; indifferent **stolidly** (adv.)

488. **stringent** (adj.) strict; severe; stern; harsh; austere **stringently** (adv.)

489. **subside** (v.) diminish; lessen; abate; wane; dwindle; recede; weaken

490. **subsist** (v.) exist; live; survive; keep going; manage to get by **subsistence** (n.)

491. **succinct** (adj.) concise; pithy; terse

492. **sullen** (adj.) hostile; morose; dour; surly; disconsolate; gloomy; glum

493. **supercilious** (adj.) arrogant; haughty; pompous; disdainful; scornful

494. **superficial** (adj.) insincere; shallow; artificial; phony **superficially** (adv.)

495. **superfluity** (n.) surplus; surfeit; plethora; glut **superfluous** adj.

496. **supersede** (v.) supplant; replace; surpass; overtake

497. **surfeit** (n.) superfluity; plethora; surplus; glut

498. **surreptitious** (adj.) secret; hidden; covert; clandestine; stealthy

499. **susceptible** (adj.) vulnerable; able to be harmed or affected **susceptibility** (n.)

500. **synoptic** (adj.) brief; abridged; concise; succinct; pithy

501. **taint** (n.) stain; blemish; blot; flaw **taint** (v.)

502. **tamper (with)** (v.) interfere; meddle; tinker

503. **tantalizing** (adj.) alluring; attractive; tempting; enticing **tantalize** (v.) **tantalizingly** (adv.)

504. **tarnish** (v.) defame; sully; taint; embarrass **tarnished** (-ed adj.)

505. **taunt** (v.) tease; criticize; insult; verbally abuse; sneer; bully **taunt** (n.)

506. **tedious** (adj.) boring; dull; dreary; humdrum **tedium** (n.) **tediously** (adv.)

507. **teeming (with)** (-ing adj.) full; crowded; brimming; swarming; packed

508. **temerity** (n.) audacity; boldness; nerve

509. **temper** (v.) moderate; mitigate; alleviate; assuage; soothe; calm; placate

510. **template** (n.) pattern; model; prototype; guide

511. **tendentious** (adj.) argumentative; confrontational; biased; opinionated

512. **timorous** (adj.) timid; fearful; apprehensive; craven; afraid

513. **treacherous** (adj.) perfidious; disloyal; dishonest; deceitful **treachery** (n.)

514. **trivial** (adj.) unimportant; minor; insignificant; inconsequential; petty; trifling; nugatory **triviality** (n.) **trivialize** (v.)

515. **truncate** (v.) cut; shorten; abbreviate; <u>abridge</u>; trim; pare; slash
516. **tumultuous** (adj.) <u>turbulent</u>; troubled; stormy; unsettled; tempestuous; <u>hectic</u> *tumult* (n.)
517. **undermine** (v.) weaken; destabilize; damage; undercut
518. **underscore** (v.) emphasize; stress; highlight; accentuate
519. **unfathomable** (adj.) difficult to understand or measure; incomprehensible
520. **unfettered** (adj.) free; liberated; unbound; unencumbered
521. **unscathed** (adj.) unharmed; unhurt; safe; undamaged
522. **untoward** (adj.) unfortunate; unpleasant; troublesome; problematic; <u>invidious</u>
523. **unwonted** (adj.) unusual; unexpected; anomalous; atypical; rare
524. **upbeat** (adj.) positive; cheerful; optimistic; happy
525. **usurp** (v.) take by force; seize; supplant; wrest; displace; arrogate *usurpation* (n.)
526. **vehement** (adj.) passionate; heated; vigorous; furious; <u>zealous</u>; <u>ardent</u>; intense *vehemence* (n.) *vehemently* (adv.)
527. **verisimilitude** (n.) authenticity; realism; plausibility; credibility; truth
528. **vatic** (adj.) <u>prescient</u>; prophetic; predictive; foreseeing; oracular
529. **viable** (adj.) <u>feasible</u>; workable; doable; possible; practicable; achievable *viability* (n.)
530. **vigilant** (adj.) watchful; attentive; alert; <u>wary</u> *vigilance* (n.)
531. **vilify** (v.) criticize; malign; <u>denigrate</u>; <u>disparage</u>; criticize; pillory; <u>belittle</u> *vilification* (n.)
532. **virulent** (adj.) dangerous; deadly; destructive; <u>pernicious</u>; malignant *virulence* (n.) *virulently* (adv.)
533. **vitiate** (v.) make something inoperable; cancel; negate; annul; invalidate
534. **vociferous** (adj.) loud; vocal; <u>voluble</u>; strident; <u>raucous</u> *vociferously* (adv.)
535. **voluble** (adj.) <u>verbose</u>; talkative; <u>garrulous</u>; <u>loquacious</u>; <u>prolix</u>
536. **waive** (v.) give up; not claim; abandon; relinquish; forego *waiver* (n.)
537. **wax** (v.) grow; increase in size; fill out; develop; swell *waxing* (-*ing* adj.)
538. **wheedle** (v.) coax; <u>cajole</u>; inveigle; persuade; entice
539. **yen** (n.) desire; longing; urge; craving
540. **zenith** (n.) peak; tip; summit; acme; crest; <u>apex</u>